BELIEVING
Jesus

STUDY GUIDE + STREAMING VIDEO

BELIEVING Jesus

A Journey Through the Book of ACTS

STUDY GUIDE + STREAMING VIDEO
EIGHT SESSIONS

Lisa Harper & Annie F. Downs

HarperChristian Resources

Believing Jesus Study Guide
© 2015 by Lisa Harper

Requests for information should be addressed to:
HarperChristian Resources, 3900 Sparks Dr. SE, Grand Rapids, Michigan 49546

ISBN 978-0-310-14611-7 (softcover)

ISBN 978-0-310-14612-4 (ebook)

Published in association with the literary agency of Alive Communications, Inc. www.alivecommunications.com.

HarperChristian Resources titles may be purchased in bulk for church, business, fundraising, or ministry use. For information, please e-mail ResourceSpecialist@ChurchSource.com.

First Printing June 2015 / Printed in the United States of America

Contents

How to Use This Guide

GROUP SIZE

The *Believing Jesus* study is designed to be experienced in a group setting such as a Bible study, Sunday school class, or any small group gathering. After viewing each video together, members will participate in a group discussion. Ideally, discussion groups should be no larger than twelve people. If the total number of participants in your group is much larger, consider breaking into two or more groups.

MATERIALS NEEDED

Participants should each have a copy of the study guide, which includes video notes, small group discussion questions, and daily personal studies to deepen learning between sessions. Participants are also strongly encouraged to have a copy of the *Believing Jesus* book. Reading the book alongside the curriculum provides even deeper insights that make the journey richer and more meaningful. The videos for each session are available via streaming and can be accessed by following the instructions on the inside front cover, or as a DVD sold separately.

TIMING

The time notations for each section indicate the *actual* time of video segments and the *suggested* time for each activity or discussion. Adhering to the suggested times will enable you to complete each session in about one hour. If you have additional time, you may wish to allow more time for discussion and activities, thereby expanding your group's meeting time to an hour and fifteen minutes or an hour and a half. If you are also having refreshments and a time of sharing prayer requests, figure in another thirty minutes.

FACILITATION

Each group should appoint a facilitator who is responsible for starting the video and keeping track of time during discussions and activities. Facilitators may also read questions aloud and monitor discussions, prompting participants to respond and ensuring that everyone in the group has the opportunity to participate.

BETWEEN-SESSIONS PERSONAL STUDY

You can maximize the impact of the course with additional study between the group sessions. Carving out about two hours total for personal study between meeting times will enable you to complete both the book and between-sessions studies by the end of the course. For each session, you may complete the personal study all in one sitting or spread it out over a few days (for example, working on it a half hour a day on four different days that week). NOTE: If you are unable to finish (or even start!) your between-sessions personal study, still attend the group study video session. We are all busy, and life happens. You are still wanted and welcome at the group even if you don't have your "homework" done.

The Declarations That Define Us

(LUKE 24:1–53; ACTS 1:1–26)

INTRODUCTION

Fear and disillusionment. Courage and commitment. Intense emotion and unbridled passion. The ultimate risk of life in exchange for undeserved grace and a treasured spot in eternity. An example for billions of people who would follow the same road centuries and millennia later. An all-out quest by a growing number of believers to risk everything to spread Jesus Christ's message around the world. The Book of Acts. Wow.

FROM THE *BELIEVING JESUS* VIDEO

Yes, that's it. That is the book we are about to dig into for the next eight weeks, and it embodies all of those things.

This study is called *Believing Jesus*, because from Acts 1:1 to 28:31, believing Jesus is the core value that marked every believer in the first church. At the end of this journey together, not only will you have studied an amazing book of the Bible, but you will also see how God supernaturally orchestrated the events in Scripture—from the Old Testament to the New Testament—to bring about the message of salvation that the early believers preached in the book of Acts. You will also see how so much of the gospel that is preached in Acts, and continues to be preached today, has had such a profound impact on our culture.

When you choose to believe Jesus—and *act* on those beliefs—things begin to shift, lives change, and the world is never the same. The stories you read on every page of the book of Acts begin to become your own. So let's journey together through the stories of the first church—the first gathering of "The Way" (as Christianity was called back then)—and see what kind of wild adventures await those who truly *believe* Jesus.

WELCOME (5 MINUTES)

Welcome to the first session of *Believing Jesus: A Journey Through the Book of Acts*. If you or any of your fellow group members do not know one another, take a little time to introduce yourselves. Next, to get things started, discuss the following question:

The book of Acts is about choosing risk over comfort. What are some examples of doing that in our everyday lives?

VIDEO TEACHING (21 MINUTES)

Play the video teaching segment for Session 1. As you watch, use the following outline to record any thoughts or concepts that stand out to you.

Notes

The book of Acts is not "relaxing"—it is a wild, adventurous, and risk-taking kind of book.

Luke, a first-century physician, wrote both the gospel that bears his name and the book of Acts. He is the only known non-Jewish (or "Gentile") writer in the Bible.

The gospel of Luke and the book of Acts were originally one book and were meant to be read as two parts of the same story. The gospel of Luke ends with the story of Jesus' resurrection, which sets up the events that follow in Acts.

Three days after Jesus' physical death, Mary Magdalene—a devoted follower of Christ whom Jesus had healed completely of demons—went to the tomb and discovered it empty. She talked to a man she at first thought was the gardener but then realized was Christ. She went back to tell the disciples that Jesus was alive, but they thought it was an "idle" tale.

Luke tells us that Jesus didn't immediately go back to heaven after his resurrection but hung out on the earth for forty days. During this time, the Gospels record ten separate occurrences of Jesus appearing to the disciples and to more than a hundred people.

In Acts 1, Luke tells us that before Jesus went up (or "ascended") into heaven, he made two declarative statements to his followers: (1) *they would receive power from the Holy Spirit,* and (2) *they would be his witnesses.* These statements became the foundation of the early church and the scaffolding that frames the rest of the New Testament.

Jesus didn't qualify these statements. He said that *everyone* who puts their hope in him would receive the power of the Holy Spirit, and this power would compel them to be his witnesses and impact the world around them.

If we could just rest in the reality that Jesus loves us—that we have been given power from the Holy Spirit and can be his witnesses to this lost and dying world—it will change everything.

SMALL GROUP DISCUSSION (30 MINUTES)

Take some time with your group members to discuss what you just watched and explore these concepts in Scripture.

1. Why is it significant that Luke, the writer of Acts, was a Gentile?

2. What does Luke tell us about Mary Magdalene? Why was she so committed to Jesus?

3. Why didn't the disciples believe Mary and the other women when they told them that Jesus had risen from the dead?

4. What was Peter's reaction to the news? What do we learn about him in Luke 24?

5. What kind of kingdom did the disciples expect Jesus to bring? How was that different from what he actually brought?

6. Why are Jesus' two declarations in Acts 1 — that those who follow him would receive power from the Holy Spirit and be his witnesses — so central to our faith?

7. When you hear "receive the power from the Holy Spirit," what does that mean to you? What qualification did Jesus make about those who could receive this power?

8. What would it look like in your life today to be Jesus' witness to this world?

INDIVIDUAL ACTIVITY (5 MINUTES)

Read or skim through some of the gospel of Luke, the book that shares an author with Acts. What stories of Jesus on earth are most interesting to you? Before the crucifixion and resurrection, what miracles stand out to you? Write down which stories are your favorites.

CLOSING PRAYER

God, thank you for your written Word. We are grateful for people like Dr. Luke who took time to write down details about the life of Jesus and the early church. Give us ears to hear your truths in the pages of Acts and eyes to see what it looks like to believe Jesus.

RECOMMENDED READING

Read chapter 1, "The Cost of Discipleship," in *Believing Jesus*. Use the space below to write down any notes or any questions you want to bring to the next meeting.

Between-Sessions Personal Study

Reflect on the content covered in the Session 1 group study by exploring the following material from the Bible and from *Believing Jesus*. Before you begin, answer these questions:

- What are you hoping to gain from this study?

- What are some things you already know about the book of Acts?

- What do you want to know more about?

- What would it look like for you to *really* believe Jesus today?

Day 1: Welcome to Acts

As Lisa mentioned in the video, Acts is written by Dr. Luke, who also authored the gospel of Luke. Together, the books take up about one-fourth of the New Testament! Dr. Luke's books were well-trusted at the time of their writing, and they still are today. The interesting viewpoint that Dr. Luke brings to his writing is that he is a Gentile, not a Jew. This means that the lens through which he sees Jesus and all the disciples is significantly different than most of the other New Testament authors, such as Paul or Peter in their letters.

Read **Luke 1:1–4**. How do we know we can trust Dr. Luke's writings? Why did he choose to write these books?

Read **Acts 1:1–2**. What does Luke say he wrote about in his first book? Why does he take time to connect the two books for his readers?

Read **Luke 24:13–49**. This passage records one of Jesus' post-resurrection appearances to his followers. What did Jesus say to these disciples after asking them what they were discussing (verses 25–26)? Why didn't they believe it was really him (verse 41)?

What did Jesus do to help them believe (verse 45)? What do you think this means?

Whom did Jesus say he would send to them? What did he ask them to do (verse 49)?

In the space below, write a prayer asking Jesus to open your mind—just as he did for the two disciples on the road to Emmaus—so you will be able to understand the Scriptures in a deeper way than ever before.

Day 2: Mary from Magdala

When it comes to dating and relationships, one question teenagers (and even more so, youth leaders) often ask is, "Do you think young men and young women can be *friends*?"

It's quite funny, honestly. When we watch preschoolers on the playground, we encourage them to play together, to share, to be nice to the other children in the sandbox—not just the ones of the same sex. But then the hormones kick in, and we adults get VERY NERVOUS that allowing teenage boys and teenage girls to be friends will end badly.

But just look at Mary Magdalene and Jesus. What we read about them in the gospels occurred when Jesus was in his early thirties—and these two young adults have a beautiful friendship from start to finish. Mary must have really mattered to Jesus, as he let her into his inner circle. (As Lisa mentioned in the video, Mary was also the first person to whom Jesus appeared after his resurrection.) In addition, she must have mattered to our friend Dr. Luke, as he was the one who introduced us to her.

Let's look back at the day Jesus and Mary met. Read **Luke 8:1–3**. What does this passage say about Mary's life before meeting Christ?

A widespread rumor, circulating as early as the fourth century AD, said that our dear Mary was a prostitute. This seems to have happened because readers merged her with the "sinful woman" in Luke 7:36–50, whose story immediately precedes Luke's first mention of Mary Magdalene, but there is actually no scriptural basis for this claim. In fact, many historians and theologians believe that Mary's affliction was illness or disease, as opposed to any form of sinfulness—yet so many of us have assumed her sin and labeled her a prostitute.

In what ways can you relate to Mary? Has anyone ever assumed they knew what you were going through? Explain.

Although Mary Magdalene traveled with Jesus for years, only Luke mentions her at this point. (She gets a tiny shout-out in Mark 16:9, but it is in regard to the resurrection of Christ.) This gives us the opportunity to do some assuming. Why do you think Mary Magdalene stood out to Luke? Why did he find it necessary to write about her in his gospel account?

All four gospel writers—Matthew, Mark, Luke, and John—tell of Mary Magdalene being present at the crucifixion (see Matthew 27:55–56, Mark 15:40–41, Luke 23:47–49, and John 19:25–27; note that in Luke's account, she is included in "the women" who followed him from Galilee). What does it say to you that Mary is mentioned in all four accounts?

Read **John 20:1–18.** Why do you think Mary went alone to the tomb?

When did Mary recognize Jesus? Why did she cry out when she heard her name?

In John 10:3, Jesus said, "The gatekeeper opens the gate for [the shepherd], and the sheep listen to his voice. He calls his own sheep by name and leads them out." How does it make you feel to know that Jesus also calls you by name?

What a beautiful model of a true friendship. Jesus loved Mary; Jesus trusted Mary; Jesus called Mary by name.

Day 3: When Jesus Showed Up

Showing up matters. When we show up for someone, it means we care, we notice, we are FOR them. We get to choose how to spend our twenty-four hours in a day—and so did Jesus. So it is important for us to notice the choices he made and the people he chose to see after his resurrection and before his ascension into heaven. Let's take a look today at ten specific instances recorded in the Bible when Jesus showed up for someone and why they mattered to him.

(1) Read **Mark 16:9–11**. To whom did Jesus appear? Why do you think Jesus appeared to this person first? Why did it matter to this person that Jesus showed up?

(2) Read **Matthew 28:8–10.** What does it say to you that Jesus appeared first to women? What are some emotions you imagine these women must have felt right then?

(3) Read **Luke 22:54–62.** What did Peter do on the night of Jesus' crucifixion? Given this, why do you think it mattered to Peter that Jesus showed up for him (see Luke 24:34)? Why do you think there is so little mention of their interaction?

(4) On Day 1 of the personal study, you read Luke 24:13–49. To whom did Jesus first appear in this passage? Why do you think he just showed up and walked along the road with these two unnamed individuals? Remember that Jesus was guiding them, but they didn't recognize him. In what ways has that happened in your life?

(5) To whom did Jesus appear next in verses 36–49? What is the first thing Jesus said to them? Why do you think their "joy and amazement" (verse 41) caused unbelief in them?

(6) Read **John 20:26–31**. To whom did Jesus appear? Why did it matter to this man that Jesus showed up? Note that a week had passed between the time the disciples first saw Jesus and when this disciple saw him. What would you guess was going on with Jesus during that time?

(7) Read **John 21:1–14**. To whom did Jesus appear? Why does it matter that Jesus showed up for these men while they were out doing their job? What was significant about what Jesus did for them?

(8) Read **Matthew 28:16–17**. To whom did Jesus appear? What was the purpose of this particular appearance? What did Jesus command these men to do? Why did it matter that they knew Jesus *was* with them and *would be* with them?

(9) Read **1 Corinthians 15:6**. To whom did Jesus appear? Note that this is the only place in Scripture where this number is mentioned—and it is such a short passing note! Why do you think Jesus chose to gather these people together and speak to them during this forty-day window?

(10) Read **Mark 6:3** and **1 Corinthians 15:7**. To whom did Jesus appear? What was this person's relationship to Christ? Why is this significant?

Of these ten documented appearances before Jesus' ascension, which one stands out most to you? Why?

Day 4: You Will Receive Power

There are two declarations that Jesus made in Acts 1. What are those two declarations? (Note: Both are listed in verse 8.)

Today we are going to focus on the first declaration: "You will receive power when the Holy Spirit comes on you." Throughout Dr. Luke's writing, we see what it looks like when the Holy Spirit comes on someone, and this gives us some context to figure out exactly what that power is. There are many other examples in the Old and New Testaments (for instance, David in Psalm 55, and all throughout the Gospels), but we will focus today on Luke and Acts.

Read **Luke 1:11–18**. What did the angel say that John the Baptist would be able to do when he was filled with the Holy Spirit?

Read **Luke 1:29–35**. What did the angel say would happen to Mary as a result of being filled by the Holy Spirit?

Read **Luke 1:39–41.** What happened when Elizabeth was filled with the Holy Spirit? What did she do in response to what Mary told her?

Read **Luke 1:67–79.** What was Zechariah able to do after being filled?

Read **Luke 2:25–27.** What three things was Simeon able to do after he was filled?

Read **Acts 2:1–4.** What did the followers in Jerusalem see when the Holy Spirit came down? What were they able to do when filled with the Holy Spirit?

Read **Acts 4:8–12.** How did Peter respond to the Sanhedrin (the Jewish religious elite) after he was filled with the Holy Spirit?

Read **Acts 7:54–56.** What was Stephen able to see after being filled with the Holy Spirit? What happened next?

Which of these instances most resonates with you? Why?

How have you seen the Holy Spirit bring power to you? In what situation in your life would you like to see the power of the Holy Spirit?

As you continue to read the book of Acts during this study, notice the places where the power of the Holy Spirit causes someone to do, say, act, or believe something. We can claim all these benefits and power moments in our own lives too!

Day 5: You Will Be My Witnesses

Today we are going to focus on the second declaration made by Jesus in Acts 1:8: "You will be my witnesses in Jerusalem, and in all Judea and Samaria, and to the ends of the earth."

Read **Matthew 28:18–20.** Where did Jesus tell his disciples to go and make other disciples?

Jesus was speaking to the disciples while they were in Jerusalem. In the map provided, put a star over Jerusalem. While standing in that very city, Jesus told his disciples to be his witnesses there, in Judea, and in Samaria. Draw a circle around all of Judea, and then draw an arrow from Jerusalem to Samaria.

The disciples would have heard these instructions differently than we do. They knew these places very well, and they knew exactly where Jesus was telling them to go. In the columns below, match where each of these places relate in your world:

your town   all the ends of the earth

your state   Samaria

your region   Jerusalem

the world   Judea

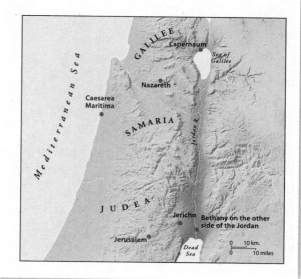

When Jesus asks us to be his witnesses—telling people who he is, what he has done, and how he has changed our lives—he isn't just asking us to go on mission trips or think about the people across the globe. As with his disciples, he is asking us to be his witnesses right where we are and in the places we already know. What would it look like for you to likewise be a witness for Jesus in your town?

In your state?

In your region?

In the world?

Earth, Wind, and Celestial Fire

(Acts 2:1 – 13)

INTRODUCTION

"When the day of Pentecost came, they were all together in one place. Suddenly a noise like a strong, blowing wind came from heaven and filled the whole house where they were sitting. They saw something like flames of fire that were separated and stood over each person there" (Acts 2:1–3).... Although it wasn't his debutant party, you have to admit the Holy Spirit made a pretty dramatic entrance here. It was complete with the special effects of wind and fire, which are both symbolically revelatory—wind is a powerful, invisible force and fire is a powerful, purifying force. I can only imagine the collective wide-eyed stares and windblown coiffures the Holy Spirit's arrival caused.

FROM *BELIEVING JESUS*

M any of us (well, at least many of us who are of a certain age!) grew up reading Nancy Drew books. Something about the mystery of what would happen next—what was actually in that box in the barn, the identity of the man in the trench coat—was irresistible.

We were built to be intrigued by mystery. It does something to our insides, makes us come alive, and brings excitement. And as we keep reading the book of Acts, we will see the mysterious ways of God, particularly in the Holy Spirit. It's okay to feel that the Holy Spirit works in some pretty mysterious ways—he does! As we explore Acts 2 and study the different attributes of the Holy Spirit, we come across some eyebrow-raising activities, to be sure. But just because something is mysterious doesn't make it untrue or ungodly. Walk bravely into this session! The Holy Spirit is a fun kind of mystery!

WELCOME (5 MINUTES)

Welcome to the second session of *Believing Jesus: A Journey Through the Book of Acts.* To get things started, discuss the following question:

What are some words you would use to describe the Holy Spirit?

VIDEO TEACHING (19 MINUTES)

Play the video teaching segment for Session 2. As you watch, use the following outline to record any thoughts or concepts that stand out to you.

Notes

Two-way communication is critical when it comes to our relationship with God, and the Holy Spirit is our way to have that communication.

Ontological equality says that God exists in three persons (God the Father, Jesus the Son, and the Holy Spirit), each person is fully God, and there is only one God. The persons are equal in value but different in function.

God the Father planned the redemption of man. Jesus the Son accomplished the redemption of man. The Holy Spirit affirms and applies the redemption of man.

In Acts 2, we receive many insights into the work and the person of the Holy Spirit. The Holy Spirit comforts us, convicts us, and frees us.

Paul describes the Holy Spirit in Romans 8:14 and reveals that the Holy Spirit has applied our redemption through Jesus.

In John 14:15, Jesus uses the word *paraclete* to describe the Holy Spirit. It means helper, advocate, one who comes alongside and helps us.

Remember, even when life is hard, you have the right to call on God the Father—to call on the Holy Spirit—to be your helper.

SMALL GROUP DISCUSSION (30 MINUTES)

Take some time with your group members to discuss what you just watched and explore these concepts in Scripture.

1. What are the differences among the three persons of the Trinity? How do you see their unique functions as being important in your life?

2. Think about the Holy Spirit's behavior and the experiences of the new Christians in Acts 2. What part of the story is most exciting to you? What part is a little weird, mysterious, or terrifying?

3. What specifically stood out to you as you read about and pictured this early gathering?

4. In John 14, why did Jesus make sure to tell his disciples about the Holy Spirit?

5. When have you needed the Holy Spirit in the past? When you prayed and asked for help, as Lisa did, how did God show up for you?

6. What attribute of the Holy Spirit speaks to your life today? Why that attribute?

7. How do you need the Holy Spirit to help you where you are *right now?*

8. What has the Holy Spirit whispered to you lately? How have you responded?

INDIVIDUAL ACTIVITY (5 MINUTES)

Spend a few minutes alone to connect with the Holy Spirit. Ask him to lead you, help you, guide you, or free you—whatever it is that you need. Then take time to listen. What is the Holy Spirit saying to you today?

CLOSING PRAYER

Lord Jesus, thank you for the Holy Spirit. Thank you for a Helper who is always with us and who reminds us we are loved and seen. Help our ears to hear and our eyes to be open to see the Holy Spirit moving and acting on our behalf and speaking to us regularly. Teach us, Holy Spirit, about your ways and your power as we seek to live a life more connected with our triune God.

RECOMMENDED READING

Read chapter 2, "Earth, Wind, and Celestial Fire," in *Believing Jesus*. Use the space below to write down any notes or any questions you want to bring to the next meeting.

Between-Sessions Personal Study

Reflect on the content covered in the Session 2 group study by exploring the following material from the Bible and from *Believing Jesus*.

Day 1: The Holy Spirit Hovers

> *This was not the Holy Spirit's first rodeo. The Holy Spirit has actually been here since the beginning of time.... We just read about him more in the New Testament because he gets more press in the New Testament. And frankly, I think we need him more in New Testament culture.*
>
> FROM THE *BELIEVING JESUS* VIDEO

We're diving into deep waters early. The Holy Spirit, the equal third part of the Trinity, is mysterious, powerful, known, and unknown. As we studied in Session 1, Day 4, we receive power when he comes on us—so we already know the power he brings. But let's back up, as Lisa mentioned, and meet the Holy Spirit as he is introduced in the Bible. God makes no mistakes—where and when stories are told are intentional moves by an excellent Author—so let's look at this first mention of the Holy Spirit.

Read **Genesis 1:1–2.** Who is the first member of the Trinity mentioned? What does this passage say about him?

Who is the second member of the Trinity mentioned? What does this passage say he was doing?

Okay, this is the fun part. Get ready. The word for *hover* in the original Hebrew is *rachap*. It means to hover, to soar, or to fly. What's interesting is that this word describing how the Holy Spirit behaves appears only two other places in the Bible. (Now rub your hands together real quick, like you're about to dive into something awesome, because you are.) One of these occurrences is Deuteronomy 32:10–11, where Moses is singing a song about how God takes care of Israel. Read these verses and circle the translation of the English word for *rachap* below:

> In a desert land he found him,
>   in a barren and howling waste.
> He shielded him and cared for him;
>   he guarded him as the apple of his eye,
> like an eagle that stirs up its nest
>   and hovers over its young,
> that spreads its wings to catch them
>   and carries them aloft.

The same word in the second verse of the Bible that describes the Holy Spirit's behavior over the earth is used in this passage to describe how God cares for his people in a protective way—like an eagle (who flies and soars) caring for its young. How cool is that? Now hold onto your feathers, we're going deeper.

Read **Genesis 8:6–12.** What happened when Noah sent out the raven to find dry land? What happened when he sent out the dove?

Read **Luke 3:21–22.** (We studied these verses in Session 1, Day 4, so you can pop back for a refresher, if you'd like.) In what form did the Holy Spirit come down on Jesus?

The Holy Spirit came down as a dove, hovering over the river where Jesus was baptized. The subtle string tied here is one not to be missed. From the first pages of the Bible—and throughout the Scripture—we are told the same thing about the Holy Spirit, often using the same picture. The Holy Spirit *hovers*. He wraps his wings around us. He protects.

Is this characteristic of the Holy Spirit new to you? If so, how does it make you feel? If not, consider a time you relied on this particular truth in the past.

What does it mean to you personally that the Holy Spirit hovers over your life?

Day 2: The Holy Spirit Helps

So far, we know the Holy Spirit brings power and the Holy Spirit hovers over us. But the direct connection we each have with the Holy Spirit allows him to be our helper in everyday life. Repeatedly, when the disciples began to worry about what it would be like when Jesus left them, he would point their gaze to this very attribute of the Holy Spirit. The Holy Spirit is here to counsel us. To help us. To be with us in our time of need.

Read **John 14:15–17**. What does Jesus call the Holy Spirit in verse 16? What does he call the Holy Spirit in verse 17?

Why is it important that Jesus tells us in the same passage that the Holy Spirit is an *advocate* (or *helper* or *counselor*) and the *Spirit of truth*?

The original Greek word John uses for *advocate* is *paraclete*. It means to comfort, to console, to call to one's aid; it also refers to a mediator or advocate, similar to how we use the word today. The Greek word for *spirit* is *pneuma*, and it means wind, breath, or spirit. In the following passages, write down the English word used for these Greek terms:

John 14:26: "But the _____, the Holy Spirit, whom the Father will send in my name, will teach you all things and will remind you of everything I have said to you."

John 15:26: "When the _____ comes, whom I will send to you from the Father—the Spirit of truth who goes out from the Father—he will testify about me."

John 16:7b: "Unless I go away, the _____ will not come to you; but if I go, I will send him to you."

Acts 1:8: "You will receive power when the Holy _____ comes on you; and you will be my witnesses in Jerusalem, and in all Judea and Samaria, and to the ends of the earth."

Acts 2:4: "All of them were filled with the Holy _____ and began to speak in other tongues as the Spirit enabled them."

Acts 2:38: "Repent and be baptized, every one of you, in the name of Jesus Christ for the forgiveness of your sins. And you will receive the gift of the Holy _____."

Although John uses the word *paraclete* and Dr. Luke uses the word *pneuma,* they refer to the exact same person: the Holy Spirit. What are some words that come to mind when you think of an *advocate* or *counselor*? What comes to mind when you think of *spirit*?

What does it mean to you that the Holy Spirit is here to help you? To be an advocate for you? To counsel you?

Day 3: The Holy Spirit Convicts

Conviction. Ick. It's that feeling in your gut when you are just a tad off center. It's that prickly sensation in your heart when you've let the wrong thing slip off your tongue or you've looked the right choice in the face and turned the other way.

Most of us equally love and hate conviction. We hate it for all the reasons listed above. Blech. But we love it because every good parent corrects their child. We love it because it reminds us that we matter to Someone. It says to us that there is a better way and it is right in front of our eyes.

The Holy Spirit, who is the Spirit of truth—who counsels us, hovers over us, and fills us with power—also loves us enough to put a quiet hand on our shoulder when we need to change course, get forgiveness, or run in the opposite direction of sin.

Read **John 16:5–16**. In verse 8, Jesus says the Holy Spirit will convict us in regard to three things. What are they?

Let's look at each of these three things. In verse 9, why does Jesus say the Holy Spirit will convict us about *sin*? What do you think that means? If someone doesn't know Jesus (as it says in verse 9), why is it important for the Holy Spirit to convict him or her of sin?

In verse 10, why does Jesus say the Holy Spirit will convict us about *righteousness*? What qualities do people tend to think of as making a person righteous? What standard does God require for a person to be truly righteous?

In verse 11, Jesus says the Holy Spirit will convict us about *judgment*. This conviction is to remind us that in the end, those who stand with Christ receive eternal life, while those who do not will not. How does this conviction play out when you think of your friends and family who do not yet know Christ?

The Holy Spirit's conviction is a gift to us. When our hearts aren't connected with Jesus and we start forgetting what he has done, the Spirit convicts us of our *sin*. When it comes to *righteousness* and righteous living, now that Jesus isn't on earth, we need the Holy Spirit to convict us to live righteously. And *judgment*? We should each remember, often, to pray for those we love who do not yet know Christ. We should pray that the Holy Spirit's conviction will fall on them and bring them into a knowledge of who Jesus is and what he has done for them.

Day 4: The Holy Spirit Frees

The Holy Spirit functions in many areas of our lives, consistently drawing us nearer to the Father and nearer to the kind of people we actually want to be. As we discussed yesterday, the Holy Spirit is the one who convicts us, and yet—at the same time—he is the one who brings freedom. Only our God could simultaneously point out our wrongs and set us free from them.

Read **2 Corinthians 3:17**. What does Paul say is present where the Spirit of the Lord is?

Read **Romans 6:15–18**. From what have we been set free?

Now read **John 8:32**. What does Jesus say the truth brings? Remember from Day 2 that the Holy Spirit is the *Spirit of truth*. If this is the case, what does it look like for him to set you free?

Jesus knew what he was doing! He knew what he was telling us. He wanted us to see these kinds of links. He wanted to make sure we knew that it is truth that sets us free, and we know that truth through the revelations brought by the Holy Spirit, the Spirit of truth.

Where we find our freedom matters. We are all looking for it. We are all hoping to be free and to be given release from the difficulties of this life. We turn to a lot of places, to a lot of things or people or vices, and we feel as if that is freedom. But the Bible says that where the Spirit of the Lord is, *there* is freedom.

There. And only there.

And we know that the Holy Spirit hovers over us, so wherever we are, we can invite the Holy Spirit to hover his freedom over our lives.

How would your life be different if you were truly free?

What is keeping you from such freedom?

Read **Romans 8:1–2** and copy it below. Then underline "no condemnation" and "the Spirit who gives life sets you free."

This is the truth. The Holy Spirit has set us free.

Day 5: The Holy Spirit Confirms

To *confirm* is to prove true and remind. Now, your memory and ability to retain everything buzzing around in your head may be airtight, but most of us need all the reminders, all the confirmations, and all the help remembering that we can get. The Holy Spirit does that for us. We can add it to his list of jobs in our lives. He confirms what our spirits know is true and reminds us of truths we may forget.

Read **Romans 8:3–14**. What title does your Bible give this section of Scripture? From what you already know about the Holy Spirit, what does it look like to live through the Spirit? What are some of the things he can do for you every day?

As we journey through Acts, we read about many people who were given wisdom through the Holy Spirit. Read **Acts 6:1–8**. What was the situation that prompted the twelve disciples to appoint the men listed in verse 5? What does Luke say about Stephen?

Read **Acts 6:9–15**. Why couldn't the Jewish leaders oppose what Stephen was saying? How instead did they try to accuse him?

In response to these accusations, Stephen gave a speech that captured his understanding of the broad sweep of history that led up to the life and death of Jesus. Read **Acts 7:51–53**. Of what did Stephen, in turn, accuse his accusers of doing?

The Holy Spirit is always beside us to help us in the ways we need. But there is one last attribute to talk about this week that is special to us and important to our lives. Read **Romans 8:15–17**. To what does Paul say we are no longer slaves? Instead, what are we?

Paul says we can now call God "Abba, Father." *Abba* is the Greek version of "Daddy"—an intimate name for a father. To live life in the Spirit is to know that God is your Father—your very good and kind and loving *Abba* Daddy. To live life in the Spirit is to let the Holy Spirit remind you of that over and over again. It's a domino effect, a chain event, all the things the Holy Spirit does for us.

Use this week's study to fill in the blanks:

The Holy Spirit _____ over us all the time, like an eagle protecting its young. He _____ us in our daily lives, like a parent caring for a child. Also, like a parent disciplining his or her child, he _____ us of our sin and points us in the right direction. He sets us _____ and _____ in our hearts what we know is true—that our God is a good Daddy.

Checkered Pasts Can Make Incredible Preachers

(MARK 14:66 – 72; ACTS 2:14 – 41; 8:1 – 3; 9:1 – 22)

INTRODUCTION

It's one thing to feel guilty about doing something wrong, but it's a whole other thing to admit you're in the wrong and then be willing to do whatever it takes to get right.... So I think it's especially poignant that [Peter] gets to be the first New Testament preacher to witness thousands of others so overcome with repentance that they humbly hurled themselves at the feet of this Jesus ... his Jesus. FROM *BELIEVING JESUS*

You know those amazing, big, round sugar cookies that bakeries make where the icing on top is half chocolate and half vanilla? It's definitely a favorite treat of many.

This week, you're going to get a similar experience—one cookie with two distinct flavors. Peter and Paul. This is going to be a fun week as we look at the similarities and differences between these two world-changers.

Both were raised Jewish, both had strong personalities with a bit of a wild side, and both went down some dark, sinful paths before embarking on the fullness of their lives in Christ. But before we try to put these two dudes on the same side of the cookie, we need to recognize that they could not have been more different. Peter was a fisherman; Paul, a scholar. Peter followed Jesus; Paul imprisoned followers of Jesus. Peter entered Acts on fire for the gospel and ready to spread it to every end of the earth; Paul entered Acts as an angry Pharisee.

Two different roads led them to the place where they would become two of the most influential Christians in the history of the church. But how exactly did God use these two men, with all their flaws and issues and mistakes? It's a pretty sweet story. (Cookie joke. Get it?)

WELCOME (5 MINUTES)

Welcome to Session 3 of *Believing Jesus: A Journey Through the Book of Acts.* To get things started, discuss the following questions:

Why do we tend to have such a hard time with the sins of our past?

Why are we slow to forgive ourselves?

Why would the enemy of our souls want us to focus on our past?

VIDEO TEACHING (21 MINUTES)

Play the video teaching segment for Session 3. As you watch, use the following outline to record any thoughts or concepts that stand out to you.

Notes

Our failures do not limit our futures as Christ followers. From the beginning of the Bible, we see many people with stained pasts going on to be amazing leaders for God's kingdom.

Peter was one such individual. He went from being a shamed man to a man with gospel bravery.

Peter denied Christ three times and completely turned his back on his best friend. In spite of this, the resurrected Jesus reinstated him and reminded him of who he was meant to be.

Fifty days later, Peter gave the first sermon after Jesus ascended to heaven, and more than three thousand people were saved.

The grace of the gospel is wildly transformative. In Acts 8 and 9, we see this at work in Paul's life. He was bent on destroying Christianity until he came face to face with Jesus. Paul would go on to write more than half of the New Testament.

We can become so enthralled with the messengers of the gospel (like Peter and Paul) that we forget the message they are teaching.

There is no stain that disqualifies us from sharing the living hope of Christ with the dying world around us, nor do we deserve to be his ambassadors—it is a gift and a privilege.

SMALL GROUP DISCUSSION (30 MINUTES)

Take some time with your group members to discuss what you just watched and explore these concepts in Scripture.

1. After Peter denied Christ three times, what gave him the courage—less than two months later—to preach in front of thousands?

2. How did God transform Paul's life? In what ways did God use him to promote the message of Christ in spite of his past?

3. Which man do you relate to most—Peter or Paul? Why?

4. The Bible is full of other people God used in spite of their imperfect pasts. What characters come to mind? What mistakes did they make? How did God use them in spite of those mistakes?

5. Why it is important to focus on the message more than the messenger? In what ways can this become a problem for believers?

6. What is the danger in assuming that a mistake in your past will forever mar your future and what you can do for God? How do the stories of Peter and Paul assure you that God is never finished with you? How have you seen the grace of the gospel transform your life?

INDIVIDUAL ACTIVITY (5 MINUTES)

Write out a prayer below, thanking God for all the parts of your checkered past that he has restored and redeemed. If there are still mistakes that feel too great to give, ask the Holy Spirit to show you his redemptive plan for your past and your future.

CLOSING PRAYER

God, thank you that you always forgive, always restore, always make new. Open up doors in my life for me to be like Peter and Paul and stand up on your behalf. Help me not to be held back by my past but to be certain of your grace and your love.

RECOMMENDED READING

Read chapter 3, "Checkered Pasts Can Make Incredible Preachers," and chapter 6, "Sinners Who Would Be Saints," in *Believing Jesus*. Use the space below to write down any notes or any questions you want to bring to the next meeting.

Between-Sessions Personal Study

Reflect on the content covered in the Session 3 group study by exploring the following material from the Bible and from *Believing Jesus*.

Day 1: Nice To Meet You

As we have already discussed, the way in which God inspires a writer to tell a story in the Bible and where that story appears matters. Nothing is accidental or random. So, to begin this session's personal study, we need to take note of the ways in which Peter and Paul are introduced to us. As we will see, both men are at first called by other names—Peter was born *Simon*, and Paul was born *Saul*.

Peter

Read **Mark 1:14–18**. What was Simon's line of work? Where did Jesus find him?

What was Jesus' instruction to Simon and his brother Andrew? What do you think would make these men leave their jobs to follow someone like Jesus?

Read **Matthew 16:13–20**. What did Simon Peter know about Jesus that no one else had figured out quite yet? Why did Jesus change his name from Simon to Peter?

It's important to recognize that despite Peter often saying the wrong thing or acting impulsively, he knew who Jesus was and believed with his whole heart. Jesus knew that, and he also knew that Peter would fail him miserably. And still he built his church on Peter, the rock.

Paul

Read **Acts 7:57–60**. Where is Saul when we first meet him?

It is clear from this passage that Saul did not participate firsthand in the murder of Stephen, but he did stand there and watch as one of Peter's beloved friends and colaborers for Christ was killed for his faith.

Read **Acts 8:1–3**. What happened to the church after the stoning of Stephen?

The word used in verse 3 for "destroy"—*elymaineto* in the Greek—is used only here in the entire Bible, and it is used to describe how Saul was ravaging the church. What kind of behaviors do you think Paul was engaging in to "destroy" the church?

Two pretty different guys so far, and yet their stories will align. We will soon see how God can truly use anyone who is willing to be used by him. As Lisa states, "There is no stain that disqualifies us from sharing the living hope of Christ to the dying world around us. Nor do we deserve to be his ambassadors—it is a gift and a privilege."

Day 2: Checkered Pasts

"All have sinned and fall short of the glory of God" (Romans 3:23). No matter where we come from and no matter where we have been, we have fallen short. It's so easy for us to look across the room, across the pew, or across the street, and see the successes in other people's lives while we focus on the failures in our own. But the Bible says we *all* have sinned. We *all* have fallen short. We *all* are in need of a Savior. This was certainly true for Peter and Paul.

Peter

Read **Luke 22:31–34.** What was the first thing Jesus said to Peter? How do you picture Jesus' voice? Soft, sad, concerned?

"I have prayed for you, Simon," Jesus said next, for he knew how hard this was going to be for Peter and how hard Peter was going to be on himself when he failed. In verse 34, what was Jesus' prediction about Peter?

Read **Luke 22:54–62**. What did Peter do on the night of Jesus' crucifixion? Given this, why do you think it mattered to Peter that Jesus showed up for him (see Luke 24:34)? Why do you think there is so little mention of their interaction?

In the Session 1, Day 3 personal study, we looked briefly at the story of Peter's actions on the night of Jesus' crucifixion (Luke 22:54–62). In that passage, three different people asked Peter about Jesus. List what they said to Peter and how Peter responded to them.

Verses	What the person said	How Peter responded
54–57		
58		
59–60		

Luke 22:61 might be the most heart-wrenching verse in the Bible: "The Lord turned and looked straight at Peter." What does this tell you about how close Jesus was to Peter? Do you think he was able to hear everything Peter said?

How would you have felt if you were in Peter's place and knew your best friend had just overheard you talking badly about him? How would you have felt when Jesus made eye contact with you?

Paul

As you'll recall from the Day 1 study, Saul was present during the stoning of Stephen and immediately afterward began to try to destroy the church. "Going from house to house, he dragged off both men and women and put them in prison" (Acts 8:3).

Read **Acts 9:1–2** (but SERIOUSLY resist reading ahead! PLEASE! For drama's sake!) What kind of threats was Saul making against the Christians? Why was he going to Damascus?

Apparently, Paul had discovered all the followers of the Way that he wanted to jail and punish in his own city, so he had decided to move on to another! Heading to Damascus to round up Christians and then imprison them in Jerusalem was more than just silencing dissenters—it was a mission to destroy.

Keep this in mind as you read **1 Corinthians 15:9.** Why did Paul say he didn't even deserve to be an apostle?

Now read **1 Timothy 1:13.** What three words did Paul use to describe himself?

1.

2.

3.

All have sinned and fallen short of the glory of God.

Day 3: When Jesus Shows Up

When we left these two men yesterday—Peter and Paul, Simon and Saul—they were on level playing fields. Both had separated from Jesus, and both were lost in their own ways. And today? Today Jesus shows up. He shows up for Peter. He shows up for Paul. And both men are changed forever.

Peter

Read **John 21:15–19.** Why do you think it's significant that Jesus asked Peter three times if he loved him?

What was the last thing Jesus said to Peter in verse 19?

Think back to Day 1. Why is it important that Jesus said to Peter, "Follow me!"

It's interesting to note that John uses two different Greek words for the word *love*—*phileo* and *agape*. *Phileo* is a type of brotherly love exhibited in a close friendship. *Agape* is the most powerful, noble, and sacrificial love possible. It's almost as if Jesus was asking Peter, "Do you love me? Do you REALLY love me"

How do you think Peter felt—especially after what we read yesterday in Luke 22:61— when he got to tell Jesus to his face that he loved him?

Paul

Read **Acts 9:3–19**. Picture the look of that wide-eyed emoji you see in social media—that's how unbelievably incredible Paul's conversion story is. What a radical transformation! Nothing will get you to change your behavior like Jesus striking you blind and telling you to get your act together!

What is the first thing Jesus said to Saul (verse 4)?

What emotions do you think some of the men traveling with Saul felt (verse 7)?

What was Ananias afraid of (verse 13)? What had he heard about Saul?

How did Jesus use Ananias to show himself to Saul?

What happened to Saul in verse 17? From what you know about the Holy Spirit, what attributes does that mean Paul possessed now?

Y'all, how amazing are those two transformations? That is how Jesus works. Whether you are meeting him for the first time, like Paul, or he is restoring you to whom you really want to be, like Peter, when he shows up, it changes everything.

Day 4: Incredible Preachers

Yes, checkered pasts can make incredible preachers. It is so true in Peter and Paul's lives. Once Peter was reinstated and Jesus told him to feed his sheep, and once Paul's eyes were healed by God, they both—pretty quickly—became incredible preachers.

Peter

You previously read Peter's sermon in Acts 2, but let's focus today on the people's response. What was their initial reaction to what the Holy Spirit was doing (verses 5–13)? What was their reaction after hearing Peter's sermon (verse 41)?

Look through the section divisions for Acts 3–4 in your Bible. What three things did Peter do after delivering his sermon on the day of Pentecost?

Verses	Peter's action
Acts 3:1–10	
Acts 3:11–26	
Acts 4:1–7	

What does this say to you about the power of the Holy Spirit that Peter carried with him?

As we continue on in Acts, we regularly see Peter and his preaching make a difference. Read **Acts 10:34–44**. Knowing what you do about Peter, why did it matter to him that God doesn't show favoritism?

How did the Holy Spirit use Peter's words (verse 44)? What was the result?

The Holy Spirit repeatedly took Peter's words and used them to change the hearts of men and women.

Paul

Paul was crazy! There's just no other way to say it. Once he met Jesus and was changed, that same fiery man who was willing to travel to other cities to arrest Christians was now willing to travel the world *for* Christ. And travel he did!

Read **Acts 9:20–31**. Why were people astonished and baffled when they heard Paul (verses 21–22)? Why did the Jews want to kill him (verse 23)?

What are the four cities listed in this passage where Paul preached and ministered? What was the ultimate result for the church (verse 31)?

Paul didn't stop there. Look up the following verses in Acts 13–14. List the cities where Paul spread the gospel and give a brief summary of what happened as a result.

Verses	City	What happened there
Acts 13:6–12		
Acts 13:14–43		
Acts 14:1–7		
Acts 14:8–18		
Acts 14:20–21		

The man had hardly let the dust fall off his shoes before he was back out on the road to the next city to share about Jesus! Ultimately, he would embark on three major missionary journeys. The first is recorded in Acts 13–14; the second in Acts 15–18; and the third in Acts 18–21. (We'll read about them as we continue in our study.) And Paul mentions other cities where he ministered in his New Testament letters.

What do you think it was about Paul's conversion that made him willing to leave his old life and travel far and wide on behalf of Jesus?

Have you ever been on a mission trip—near or far? If so, where have you gone? What impact did you (and your team) make?

As you continue to read the book of Acts, take note of Peter and Paul. Don't miss their moments of ministry that weave in and out of the entire book.

Day 5: Legacy

As Lisa mentioned in the video, the legacy that Peter and Paul left behind on this planet truly cannot be measured this side of heaven. Many of the New Testament books are attributed to these men, so if nothing else, their written words continue to affect Christians for generations and generations. But their impact has stretched far beyond just the words.

Peter

We don't have the space or time to dig into everything that happened to Peter, but even in your reading of Acts—watching as Peter is arrested and then miraculously rescued from jail, and as people around him are healed and saved—you can see that his checkered past sure made for an impactful future. Yet perhaps his legacy is best captured in his own words.

Read **1 Peter 1:3–9**. How did Peter summarize the work of Jesus in his life and in the lives of all believers (verse 3)?

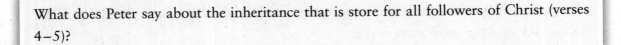

What does Peter say about the inheritance that is store for all followers of Christ (verses 4–5)?

According to the book of Acts, Peter was imprisoned for his faith in Christ (see 4:3; 5:18; 12:3–4) and even beaten (see 5:40). What does he say in his first epistle about suffering (1 Peter 1:6–7)? How does he view his suffering in light of his greater legacy in Christ?

It's widely believed that Peter died in AD 64, not long after the two letters that bear his name, 1 Peter and 2 Peter, were penned. Though his death is not described in Scripture, historians believe he was crucified head down instead of head up, because he did not feel worthy to be crucified in the same manner as Christ.

Look again at **John 21:18–19,** which we read on Day 3. What did Jesus say about Peter's death?

Picture our friend Peter at the end of his life. A man somewhere in his sixties who had traveled with Jesus, stood by his side, broken his heart, and looked him directly in the eye. A man who had been reinstated by Christ himself, had helped establish and build up the church, and had gone on for thirty years to minister on behalf of the gospel.

And then was crucified.

Sit with that for a minute. Now, based on what you have read in Acts and 1 Peter, write a few words reflecting on how the life of Peter impresses you.

Paul

You would be hard-pressed to run out of verses, stories, and information about Paul in the Bible. You could spend years studying his life, his travels, and his impact. And we are lucky enough to see where it all began—on the road to Damascus.

Unfortunately, similar to Peter, historians teach us that Paul was also killed for his faith. After all his missionary travels, sufferings, shipwrecks, and jail time, Paul wrote one final letter, which is widely believed to be the book of 2 Timothy. As you read this letter, it surely feels as if they are Paul's last words to the church.

Read **2 Timothy 4:1–8.** Think of this as Paul's last pen to paper, written from a Roman jail cell before he was killed. What did Paul say about the end of his life?

What kind of encouragement did he give Timothy?

If you were receiving this letter from your mentor, what part of his encouragement in verses 1–5 would stand out to you?

Picture our friend Paul at the end of his life. A man somewhere in his sixties who had broken Jesus' heart, had looked him in the eye, and had been miraculously changed by Christ himself. A man who had traveled for Jesus, stood up for his Lord, helped establish and build up the church, and gone on for thirty years to minister on behalf of the gospel.

And then was martyred. Killed for his faith in Jesus.

Sit with that for a minute. Now, based on what you have read in Acts and 2 Timothy, write a few words reflecting on how the life of Paul impresses you.

What is one word you would use to describe Paul's legacy? Why that word?

What is one word you would use to describe Peter's legacy? Why that word?

What is one word you would want people to use to your describe YOUR legacy? Why that word?

What's Mine Is Yours

(ACTS 2:42 – 47; 4:32 – 5:11)

INTRODUCTION

It might not be too much of a stretch to say our survival as a human race is dependent upon how well we learn to share.

FROM *BELIEVING JESUS*

———————

Annie and her college roommate had a saying: "What's mine is yours and what's yours is yours." It's a phrase they used whenever they felt the other person was being just a tad bit selfish, and it served as a good way to defuse a potential argument while still expressing their true emotions or concerns.

"Oh … so MY shoes are YOUR shoes, and YOUR shoes are YOUR shoes?"

"Yes, but MY chocolate is YOUR chocolate, and YOUR ice cream is YOUR ice cream?"

They'd keep going, in fits of laughter, until they were talking about mansions and airplanes and all manner of things that college students think adults have.

It's not a healthy long-term solution to think that way, though—as if one party is willing to share but the other isn't. It's definitely not how we model sharing to children or how we encourage adults to treat each other. Still, it's not often we find a community *built* around the idea that when someone is in need, others help—a community where those in need can feel the freedom and liberty to ask for help without shame.

We tend to lean one way or the other—"I always need help, but I have nothing to offer," or, "I don't need any help, but what I can I do for you?" However, there's another answer. There is another way.

What's mine is yours. Period.

That's the community we see in Acts, and that's the freest way to live.

WELCOME (5 MINUTES)

Welcome to Session 4 of *Believing Jesus: A Journey Through the Book of Acts*. To get things started, discuss the following questions:

What is the best part about the community in which you live?

What do you love about your neighborhood, your church, or your town?

VIDEO TEACHING (20 MINUTES)

Play the video teaching segment for Session 4. As you watch, use the following outline to record any thoughts or concepts that stand out to you.

Notes

Jesus was always motivated by mercy, not by any sanctimonious piety.

Jesus came to heal the sick, not the well. We need to acknowledge our neediness.

The Christians in Acts recognized their own appropriate neediness, which is why their community was so strong. It was a model of *healthy reciprocity*—those who were in need said so, and those who had resources to give shared them.

Healthy community exists when we likewise acknowledge *our own* appropriate neediness and are willing to share what we have with others.

Community is a system in which followers of Christ come together and realize they are better together than they are apart.

The early Christians were so dependent on Jesus that they knew how to be interdependent on each other.

Theologian Lesslie Newbigin said, "The only hermeneutic of the gospel is a congregation of men and women who believe it and live by it." We can actually understand Jesus better through the lens of community—through healthy give-and-take. A community with a healthy reciprocity is God's gift to us.

Donald Miller sums up our need for community this way: "Jesus does not want us floating through space or sitting in front of our televisions. Jesus wants us interacting, eating together, laughing together, praying together. Loneliness is something that came with the fall."

SMALL GROUP DISCUSSION (30 MINUTES)

Take some time with your group members to discuss what you just watched and explore these concepts in Scripture.

1. Think about the paralyzed man lying beside the pool in John 5. What was life like for him before he met Jesus? Why did Jesus ask him, "Do you want to get well?"

2. How would you define "appropriately weak"?

3. In what ways does our society look like the church in Acts? It what ways could it improve to be more like it?

4. Think about a need you have had in your life. How did you go about asking for help? How did you feel about asking for help?

5. Who is someone who answered the call and helped you during a time of need? What did that person do for you?

6. What can we learn from the church in Acts about "healthy reciprocity"? What would that look like in our own lives and communities?

7. What does healthy community teach us about Jesus? How does it provide a model for understanding more about Christ?

8. What would it look like if we allowed the Holy Spirit to empower us to be better friends to one another?

INDIVIDUAL ACTIVITY (5 MINUTES)

This week, call a friend and ask for help with something. Anything—to carpool, get a recipe, receive Bible study help, or just to talk through an issue or a worry. Then pick another friend to call and see how you can help him or her. Practice healthy reciprocity. Use this brief time to brainstorm and pray through ideas.

CLOSING PRAYER

God, we want to be in the kind of community that encourages healthy reciprocity. Thank you that you made humans so that we need each other and need you. Teach us, Holy Spirit, how to do community well—how to give to those who are in need and how to ask when we are the ones in need. Show us how to love each other like Jesus loves.

RECOMMENDED READING

Read chapter 4, "What's Mine Is Yours," in *Believing Jesus*. Use the space below to write down any notes or any questions you want to bring to the next meeting.

Between-Sessions Personal Study

Reflect on the content covered in the Session 4 group study by exploring the following material from the Bible and from *Believing Jesus.*

Day 1: The Church in Acts

> *The early Christians were so dependent on Jesus that they knew how to be interdependent on each other.*
>
> FROM THE *BELIEVING JESUS* VIDEO

The church in Acts was brand new. They had the opportunity to set a culture and decide what serving Christ really looked like on a day-to-day basis. We are all are born into a culture where the behaviors and systems are pretty well established. But what if they weren't? What would it look like to have no scaffolding of Christianity on which to build? That's what the original church was facing, and we can see what it looked like.

Read **Acts 2:42–47.** What stands out to you about how these believers treated each other?

In verse 46, Luke also talked about the hearts of the people in the church. What two words did he use to describe their hearts?

1.

2.

In the original Greek, the first word is *agalliasis*, which means excited, exuberant, full of joy—INTENSE joy, EXTREME joy. When have you felt such intense joy with your fellow believers?

In the original Greek, the second word is *aphelotés*, which means simplicity, uncomplicated and unencumbered, without hindrances or stumbling blocks. This is the only place in the Bible where this word is used! Why do you think Dr. Luke put "extreme joy" and "uncomplicated" together in a sentence to describe the hearts of these believers?

Joyful and *uncomplicated*. Isn't that a great way to describe our most life-giving relationships? It should be our goal to live in such a way that we create a community that reflects Christ, brings joy, and wards off complications and hindrances in the lives of others.

Day 2: Four Good Friends

> *We were created for deep connection with relatively safe people who are willing to carry us to rooftops, whip out a saw, cut a hole, and then lower us to Jesus when we need healing, like a band of brothers did for their paralyzed friend.*
>
> FROM THE *BELIEVING JESUS* VIDEO

Sometimes our community has to do for us what we cannot do for ourselves. We all experience that on a daily basis—and not just when it comes to home repairs or car issues! But on a deeper, spiritual level, we also need community—for healing, or freedom, or a touch from God that we can't achieve alone. Have you ever felt that before? Have you ever helped someone get to Jesus who couldn't get to him on their own? Have you ever been helped in that way?

Read **Luke 5:17–26.** In this story, how did the men first attempt to get their friend in front of Jesus? What went wrong? What kept them from getting to Jesus?

How did they eventually get him inside? How did Jesus respond to their efforts (verse 20)?

Why do you think Jesus forgave the man's sins *before* he healed the man's body (verse 24)?

Why does our faith matter in the lives of other people?

This story is found in two other gospel accounts: **Matthew 9:1–8** and **Mark 2:3–12**. What are some similarities in the three accounts? What are some differences that stand out?

One interesting item to note is that this incident happened in Jesus' hometown. How would it shape your understanding of the event if Jesus was friends with any of the men involved—the paralyzed man or his friends?

In many ways, these men were modeling behaviors that would, in just a few years, be the core tenets of the newly born Christian church. How does their behavior fit into the belief system and culture of the church in Acts?

Day 3: Brothers

> *We were created for deep connections with relatively safe people who are willing to sacrifice their own comfort and security for our well-being, like Jonathan did for David.*
>
> FROM THE *BELIEVING JESUS* VIDEO

If there was ever a friendship that would make an incredible tear-jerking television show, it's the friendship of David and Jonathan. Jonathan was the son of Saul, the king of Israel. David was an up-and-coming kid who was anointed to be the next king of Israel. This stat alone—that a shepherd and not the king's son was in line for the throne—is enough to predict the hatred and competition that could easily have existed between two young men.

Instead, they were the best of friends.

Read **1 Samuel 18:1–4**. How does the author describe Jonathan's love for David?

Read **Matthew 22:34–40**. What two commandments did Jesus say are the most important? How did David and Jonathan's friendship embody these commandments?

Read **1 Samuel 19:1–7**. How did Jonathan rescue his friend David?

This is when the drama really kicks up, and you're probably gonna need a tissue as you watch this friendship play out. Remember, these are real people who walked this planet, felt the same emotions we feel, and experienced joy and pain as we do. Many historians age David at around eighteen or so when he met Jonathan, while Jonathan was in his late twenties. They are two young men, best of friends, about to be separated for the rest of their days on earth.

Read **1 Samuel 20:1–42**. How did David express his worries and fears to Jonathan (verses 1–4)? How did Jonathan try to address those concerns (verses 12–17)?

Have you ever had a friend put their own well-being aside so that you would be safe? If so, what did your friend do? How did you respond?

What happened to Jonathan when he tried to intervene for David (verse 33)? What emotions did each man display (verses 34–41)? Why do you think David wept the most?

Long before the church in Acts even began, these men were modeling friendship in a deep and sacrificial way. How does Jonathan and David's behavior fit into the belief system and culture of the church in Acts?

Day 4: A Bitter Mother-in-Law

> *We were created for deep connections with relatively safe people who are willing to walk alongside us even when we're not the best company, like Ruth stuck by her bitter mother-in-law, Naomi.*
>
> FROM THE *BELIEVING JESUS* VIDEO

The beginning of the story of Ruth and her mother-in-law, Naomi, is one of great tragedy. Listen to the words of Scripture:

> A man from Bethlehem in Judah, together with his wife and two sons, went to live for a while in the country of Moab.... Elimelek, Naomi's husband, died, and she was left with her two sons. They married Moabite women, one named Orpah and the other Ruth. After they had lived there about ten years, both Mahlon and Kilion also died, and Naomi was left without her two sons and her husband (Ruth 1:1, 3–5).

In the span of ten years, Naomi attended the funerals of three men in her family. She was left alone, mourning, with her two daughters-in-law, now also widows. As a childless widow, she was among the most disadvantaged classes in the ancient world. She had no means of support and would have to live off the generosity of others. This posed an immediate problem, because she had no support system in Moab. So she made the decision to go back to Israel, to the land of her people, where she presumably had family to live with and people who could care for her.

Read **Ruth 1:6–13.** What direction did Naomi give her daughters-in-law? Why did she tell them to do this? How did they react to her words?

Why did Naomi say her loss was more bitter than Ruth and Orpah's (verse 13)?

Read **Ruth 1:14–18.** Why do you think Ruth wanted to go with Naomi? Why do you think Orpah stayed in Moab?

Read **Ruth 1:19–21.** How did Naomi describe herself? Why did she change her name to Mara?

How do you think Ruth felt when Naomi described her life as "empty"?

Think a minute about Ruth's choice and her travel companion. One would have to imagine that anyone who self-identifies as "bitter" probably isn't the most happy-go-lucky road warrior. It's about a fifty-mile trek back to Bethlehem, and they weren't in a spacious SUV. They journeyed together on foot, or maybe on camel, for days. Ruth knew an unknown land lay ahead of her, while bitter Naomi knew she was going home empty. Why do you think Ruth stayed true to her commitment in spite of Naomi's bad attitude?

Love others as you love yourself, eh? Sounds like this was a rough situation in which to live out that command. But again, as we saw with Jonathan and David and the paralyzed man with his friends, before the New Testament was lived or written—before the church in Acts was even formed—Ruth was living a life that would be welcomed in that community.

How does Ruth's behavior fit into the belief system and culture of the church in Acts?

Day 5: Friends in Ministry

Today we head back into Acts to look at the start of an interesting friendship between Paul and Barnabas. Read **Acts 4:32–36**. This is where we first meet Barnabas. What does he do in this passage?

Read **Acts 9:26–28**. We read this Scripture during the Session 3 personal study, but take a look at it again, this time focusing on Barnabas. What role did Barnabas play in Paul's life?

Read **Acts 11:19–26**. How did Luke describe Barnabas (verse 24)? Why was he sent to Antioch at first? Why did he go to Tarsus? How long did Barnabas and Paul teach in Antioch?

Read **Acts 13:1–3**. Whom did the Holy Spirit specifically set aside to do ministry together? What did the rest of the church at Antioch do for them?

Both Paul and Barnabas were welcomed into the church and became part of it, and both knew what it was like to live in a community that loved one another and met each other's needs. These two men ended up traveling together for years, teaching and training churches and church leaders. *Years.* Imagine it. There is barely a verse in Acts 13–15 where Dr. Luke doesn't say one of the men's names without the other nearby. Until one fateful day … (More about that in a later session.)

In this session's video, Lisa said, "Community is a system in which followers of Christ come together and realize we are better together than we are apart." Do you think that was true for Paul and Barnabas? Why or why not?

How do you see Paul and Barnabas's friendship reflecting the core values of the church in Acts?

Loving More People, More

(ACTS 6:1–7; 8:26–40; 10:1–11:18)

INTRODUCTION

None of us have the right to withhold God's grace from anybody else, regardless of their color, or creed, or country of origin, or ethnicity. We don't have the right to segregate people and assume that there is something they've done or something they are that could catapult them outside of the arena of salvation.

FROM THE *BELIEVING JESUS* VIDEO

———

There's a childhood song from church that Annie never understood when she was little.

"Jesus loves the little children ... all the children of the world." (She got that part.)

"Red and yellow, black and white, they are precious in his sight ..."

That's the part that always threw her off. Red and yellow? Black and white? No one matched those colors she saw in her crayon box, so what part of the world did THEY come from? Annie truly didn't get it.

As much as racism/discrimination is generations old, it is also learned. It is nurture, not nature. Kids may notice differences in people (and shout them out at embarrassing moments), but they do not know why those differences should make them better or worse than another person until they are taught that by family or culture or media.

And of course racism and discrimination aren't just about the color of skin or the texture of hair. People can be discriminated against because of their age or gender or socioeconomic class. So many things we can't control can become labels that define us.

We see Paul and Peter wrestle with this in the book of Acts as the church grew and attracted people from different walks of life. They accepted the challenge they faced two thousand years ago in their world and made a difference, and we must do the same. We can't shy away from the awkward feelings and the hard conversations that exist around this topic.

So lean in. Grab a hand. And remember we are all precious in God's sight.

WELCOME (5 MINUTES)

Welcome to Session 5 of *Believing Jesus: A Journey Through the Book of Acts*. To get things started, discuss the following questions:

Thinking about current events, how do you see racial tension and discrimination affecting our culture?

Is the current situation better or worse than it was fifty years ago? Why?

VIDEO TEACHING (16 MINUTES)

Play the video teaching segment for Session 5. As you watch, use the following outline to record any thoughts or concepts that stand out to you.

Notes

We need to be reminded that no one—regardless of their color or creed or country of origin—is less than anyone else.

Bullies aren't born—bullies are made. Hatred and bigotry are taught.

The church in Jerusalem had to deal with bigotry when, in a short amount of time, the number of believers swelled from a hundred and twenty in Acts 1, to more than three thousand in Acts 2, to five thousand in Acts 4.

Bigotry threatened to thwart what God was doing among the early Christians. They had to learn there is no color or creed that can limit people from God's grace.

In Acts 11, Peter tells of a vision he had about no longer labeling certain things clean and certain things unclean. Peter says, "Who was I that I could stand in God's way?" That phrase comes from the Greek *kóluó*, which means to withhold.

Peter's point was that no one has the right to withhold God's grace from others, regardless of their race or religious background or ethnicity. No one has the right to segregate people and assume there is something they've done or something they are that could catapult them outside the arena of salvation.

Faith in Jesus + nothing = salvation. We often try to add to that equation, but that is the fullness of the truth of the gospel.

In Revelation, it is clear that the new heaven and the new Jerusalem are a community full of different nationalities and ethnic origins, all standing equally before God and laying their crowns down before him.

SMALL GROUP DISCUSSION (30 MINUTES)

Take some time with your group members to discuss what you just watched and explore these concepts in Scripture.

1. How did the issue of race and bigotry threaten the good things God was doing in the early church? How does it threaten what God is doing today?

2. Why do people sometimes try to withhold grace from people of other cultures? What rationales do even Christ followers sometimes use as a basis for discrimination?

3. How did the Jewish peoples' history play into how they felt about other cultures? How does our history play into our views?

4. What does Peter's vision in Acts 11 tell us about how God sees all people? Why would his vision have been so startling to the Jewish believers of the early church in Acts?

5. Why was it significant that Peter was the one who had the vision of the clean and unclean animals?

6. How did God put Peter in a place where he could influence the issue of bigotry and discrimination in the early church? How does he likewise place us into positions where we can influence our communities?

7. What are some things we can do to start working toward racial reconciliation?

8. If "faith in Jesus + nothing = salvation," how does that truth bring freedom to our lives?

INDIVIDUAL ACTIVITY (5 MINUTES)

How has racial tension affected your community—if not your immediate neighborhood, then the greater area? What attempts have those in your community made for racial reconciliation? If you are not aware of any such efforts, do a little research this coming week and brainstorm some small things you could do to be a part of the healing process. Take a couple of minutes to start thinking—and praying—about that now.

CLOSING PRAYER

Lord Jesus, thank you for the lesson you give us in Acts that salvation is never faith in you plus our preferences, but rather faith in you plus nothing. Continue to remind us that grace is an all-access system and that anyone who puts his or her hope in you will be saved. Help us to live that way and truly become a family of believers. We know we can only do it through the empowering of your Holy Spirit.

RECOMMENDED READING

Read chapter 5, "Loving More People, More," in *Believing Jesus*. Use the space below to write down any notes or any questions you want to bring to the next meeting.

Between-Sessions Personal Study

Reflect on the content covered in the Session 5 group study by exploring the following material from the Bible and from *Believing Jesus*.

Day 1: The Ethiopian

You are really going to love Philip. There's just something about this guy. We first meet him in Acts 6:1–6 (along with our friend Stephen) when he is selected to be among the group of seven men chosen to oversee the daily distribution of food to those in need. It's important for us to meet Philip this way, when he is chosen to care for others. He is considered full of the Spirit and wisdom, and he must be full of compassion as well, based on the role he was commissioned to fill. Knowing this about his character, it shouldn't surprise us to see what he does in Acts 8 when he runs into a man from a different side of the tracks.

Read **Acts 8:4–8**. Where did Philip initially go to proclaim Christ? What was their response? How did it change the city?

Read **Acts 8:26–29**. What do you think was going through Philip's mind when the angel appeared to him and instructed him to head to the desert?

Have you ever had the opportunity to follow God to a place even though you didn't quite know why you were going? Explain.

We soon discover this was no average Ethiopian whom Philip encountered. What was this guy's job (verse 27)? Whom did he work for?

Philip obeyed the angel's instructions and approached the chariot. Read **Luke 10:25 – 37**. Whom does Philip remind you of in this story? (Notice this is a story featuring men of different cultures!)

To whom did Jesus tell this parable (verse 25)? Why is that significant?

In the parable, who passed by the injured man? Who stopped to care for him? Why would this have been offensive to the people hearing the story? What was Jesus trying to say?

We have to wonder if Dr. Luke was reminded of the Good Samaritan story he had told in his gospel when he was penning this portion of Acts. Read **Acts 8:30–40**. As we continue to watch Philip live out this story, we find that he too was never deterred by the man's ethnicity or status. How is Philip's behavior a good reflection of the heart of the church in Acts?

How did Philip model the truth that faith in Jesus + nothing = salvation? What happened as a result of his willingness to extend grace to this man from another culture?

When discrimination was a choice—and discrimination is ALWAYS a choice—what did Philip choose instead? Why?

Notice what happened in verse 39 after Philip baptized the eunuch: Philip disappeared. What! What do we do with that? In fact, there is biblical precedent for it—we know that when Jesus was resurrected, he would often appear in one place and then suddenly disappear to reappear in another. Dr. Luke tells us about it in Luke 24:51. But whoa, right? How interesting.

It's okay if this scene doesn't fit neatly into a box for you. It doesn't for anyone. It's mysterious and complicated and uncommon. That's okay. Let it live there, and remember that our God is a God of the miraculous and mysterious and awesome.

Day 2: Our Friend Ruth

We met Ruth in the Session 4 personal study when we saw her commitment to her sweet (well, more like bitter) mother-in-law. But it's worth taking another peek at her story of redemption to notice all the opportunities to practice discrimination.

Read **Ruth 1:22–2:3**. What time of year did Naomi and Ruth return to Bethlehem? How did Ruth and Naomi take advantage of this timing?

Read **Deuteronomy 24:19**. What three people groups did God instruct the Israelites to leave extra grain behind for?

1.

2.

3.

Notice Ruth had two strikes against her: she was a foreigner from a different land and culture, and she was also widowed and poor. (We don't know whether she was "fatherless" as well, but we do know that her father-in-law had passed away, and she now considered Naomi her only family.) She was an outsider, an alien, and there were many places where she would be unwelcome in this town.

Read **Ruth 2:4–12**. "As it turned out" (verse 3), Ruth was working in a rather interesting field. Whose field was it? How is he described (verse 1)?

What did Boaz offer her (verses 8–9)? What do you think was his motivation for doing so?

How did Ruth describe herself (verse 10)? Why was she surprised at Boaz's kindness?

Can you hear Ruth's voice, questioning and confused? *Why is this wealthy man of standing talking to me, a poor, foreign widow?* she must have thought. (Does anybody else think this could be a storyline from *Downton Abbey* or a pre-Civil War plantation movie?) How do you think his kindness made Ruth feel? What emotions would it have stirred up within her?

When discrimination was a choice—and discrimination is ALWAYS a choice—what did Boaz choose instead? Why?

The rest of the book of Ruth reads like a beautiful romance novel. Take ten minutes, grab your favorite beverage, and finish reading it. Now focus in on the events in Ruth 4:12–33, and remember who Ruth and Boaz are as you read. The two are getting married, ignoring any social improprieties or racial issues.

Fast-forward three generations and Ruth becomes the great-grandmother of a pretty important guy in the Bible. Yes, of course, Jesus!

Skim through the list of names in **Matthew 1:1–16** (don't miss verse 5!). This is the family lineage of Jesus, which traces back to a man loving a woman because of her noble character (see Ruth 3:11), not for how she looked or the money she had. What further insights does this give on how God views all people and how he wants us to treat one another?

Day 3: Cornelius

Discrimination does not discriminate. No race or culture or "texture of hair," as Lisa puts it, is safe from being treated poorly for who they are.

At the time of the church in Acts, the largest segregation between THIS side of the tracks and THAT side of the tracks was the Jews and Gentiles. Jesus was raised a Jew, and we know from the Gospels that he mainly ran with guys who were Jews and believed he was the Messiah. So when he left the earth and these Jewish men were suddenly surrounded by many different nationalities of people becoming Christ followers, it was a little off-putting for Jesus' original Jewish inner circle, to say the least.

This was especially true because Jews were careful to observe the Law and be sure to keep the "clean" clean and not touch the "unclean." The Gentiles had no such restrictions. And among those Gentile groups, one could suppose that the Roman soldiers were as off-putting as you could get, especially because they were the ones arresting people like Peter, John, and Paul. So how would Peter, a devout Jew and follower of the Law, respond when offered an invitation to come to just such a Roman soldier's house?

Read **Acts 10:1–8**. Who was Cornelius (verse 1)? Where did he live? What was his job?

What else does Luke tell us about Cornelius's character (verse 2)?

Cornelius was a centurion—and a generous one at that. He was not just *any* Roman soldier in the Italian regiment; he was the *boss*. Read **Acts 10:9–23**. What vision did God give to Peter? What was Peter's reaction to it?

What did the Holy Spirit say to Peter while he was contemplating what he had seen (verse 19)?

Read **Acts 10:24–26**. What is unusual about the exchange between Peter and Cornelius? How do you think Cornelius viewed Peter at this point?

Read **Acts 10:27–33**. Notice what Peter said in verse 28. How do his words reveal the religious discrimination he harbored?

When discrimination was a choice—and discrimination is ALWAYS a choice—what did Peter choose instead? Why?

Peter concluded, "I now realize how true it is that God does not show favoritism" (verse 34). Have you ever struggled with feeling as if God shows favoritism? Perhaps because someone got what you wanted, or because someone didn't get what you thought he or she deserved? What has been your experience with this?

Read **Acts 10:44–48**. Why were the other believers who came with Peter astonished?

What can this teach us about the power to overcome discrimination?

What does this passage also teach us about showing grace to those who show discrimination?

Unfortunately, many people are raised with some hint of discrimination in their family line, in their family stories, and in their conversations around the dinner table. However, this passage illustrates that there is always room for God to bring growth and change, wisdom and right-thinking. All we need to do is ask God to give us a mind that sees people the way he does.

Day 4: Age Doesn't Matter

At the end of John's gospel, the writer tells us, "Jesus did many other things as well. If every one of them were written down, I suppose that even the whole world would not have room for the books that would be written" (John 21:25).

Indeed, the men who wrote the Gospels undoubtedly had many stories of Jesus' life to choose from. So when we see a story mentioned in multiple accounts, our minds should perk up. It means the event caught the eyes and ears of these men so much that they all chose to include it. One such story is when people were bringing children to Jesus.

Read **Luke 18:15–17**. All week, we've focused on discrimination and the many forms it can take: racial, socioeconomic, class, career, religion. But this passage looks at it from a different angle—from a few feet lower and little more wide-eyed. Why do you think mamas and daddies were bringing their kiddos to Jesus?

Who was it that didn't want the kids around? Why were they rebuking people for bringing little ones to Jesus?

How did Jesus respond to the disciples? How did he respond to the kids?

How did Jesus say we are supposed to be like the children?

Read **Matthew 18:13–15.** Note that Luke uses the word "babies" while Matthew says "little children." Why the difference, do you think? What is similar in what Jesus said about the children in each account?

Now read **Mark 10:13–16**. What word does Mark use to describe Jesus' feelings when he saw his disciples turn away the children? How do you suppose Jesus portrayed this emotion to them?

Mark is the only gospel writer who narrowed in on Jesus' emotional response to the disciples' discrimination. The word he used in the original Greek is *aganakteó*, which, when translated, means to be angry, grieve much, or feel indignant. Why does the discrimination against children cause such a huge emotional response in Jesus?

When discrimination was a choice—and discrimination is ALWAYS a choice—what did Jesus choose instead? Why?

There is a truth here for us to grab—our age doesn't determine our nearness to Jesus. He does not turn us away for our immaturity or lack of knowledge. He does not show favoritism.

Day 5: Samaritans

Talk about a people group that was treated poorly in the Bible! The Samaritans were a tribe disliked by the Jews all the way back to 2 Kings, when they came into being. Today we will look at the source of this animosity and how it played out in the Gospels and the book of Acts.

Read **2 Kings 17:24–29**. At this point in history, the kingdom of Israel had effectively come to an end. Hoshea, the last king of Israel, made the poor choice of not paying the annual tribute to Assyria, the powerhouse in the Middle East at the time. This led to an Assyrian invasion and the enslavement of the Israelites. The Assyrian policy of the day was to resettle conquered peoples to other lands in order to break any hopes they might have of uniting and staging a rebellion. In this case, the king brought people from five different regions and settled them into the land of Samaria.

Where were the people from (verse 24)?

1.

2.

3.

4.

5.

As the peoples began to intermarry (see Ezra 9:1–2), a new tribe was created with mixed race, mixed blood, and mixed religion. However, "even while these people were worshiping the Lord, they were serving their idols" (2 Kings 17:41). Why was this a problem? Why do you think this led to issues with the Jewish people?

There's a pretty nasty history that follows between the Samaritans and the Jews. The book of Nehemiah tells us of how the Samaritans tried to stop him and the Jews from repairing the walls of Jerusalem (see 6:1–14). The Samaritans also only believed in the first five books of the Old Testament, a major affront to the Jews who believed in the fullness of the Old Testament. Bottom line, neither group liked the other. Ever. But then Jesus came along, saw all the stereotypes and discrimination, and broke down those walls.

Read **John 4:1–26**. Whom did Jesus run into at this well? What kind of woman was she?

Why do you think Jesus was kind to her? What risk would that have posed for him?

The woman was surprised Jesus would even speak to her (verse 9). Why?

This meeting actually represented double trouble for Jesus because he was a Jew and a man, and she was a Samaritan and a woman—all reasons they should not interact in public. Given this, what statement was Jesus making to this woman?

Read **John 4:39–42**. What statement was Jesus making to the people in that culture? What statement is Jesus making to us?

Now read **Acts 8:14–17**. As you will recall from Day 1, the revival that broke out in Samaria came as a result of Philip's preaching there. What was Peter and John's response to the news? What does this tell you about these two men?

What does this story tell you about whether the Holy Spirit shows favoritism?

When discrimination was a choice—and discrimination is ALWAYS a choice—what did Peter, John, and the Holy Spirit choose instead? Why?

What would it look like for *you* to be a part of breaking down the walls of discrimination? Whom could you speak to in an act of faith, believing that the Holy Spirit never shows favoritism and that Jesus longs for unity?

What can you do today to remind yourself, and the people around you, that every single person is worthy of God's affection?

The Need to Be ReGospeled

(GALATIANS 2:11 – 21; ACTS 9:26 – 27;
11:19 – 30; 15:36 – 41)

INTRODUCTION

You may be encouraged to know that Peter and Paul didn't just mess up before they became giants in Christendom ... but actually in the process of running hard after Jesus, while they were missionaries, while they were church planters. They fumbled the ball on the first-yard line, they blew it royally, they failed with flying colors.

FROM THE *BELIEVING JESUS* VIDEO

Annie tells this story:

"It isn't easy being human. I mean, I've never been anything else. I just know that there are times when I wish I wasn't so very human.

"Humans make a lot of mistakes. I make a lot of mistakes. A while ago, I borrowed an apron while cooking chicken and dumplings at a friend's house. She had, a few years before, gone to culinary school and received this apron as her course completion reward. She treasured it, and I felt honored to wear it.

"By the end of the night I had splattered chicken pieces and dumpling shrapnel all over it, so I offered to take it home to throw into the wash. And when I did? It ripped. Somehow an apron string caught in the washing machine and ripped right off the apron. I was mortified.

"That wasn't the human part. That was just an accident. The mistake was when I decided to hide what had happened. The mistake was when I tried to fix my friend's prized apron myself and never told her until she realized something was 'off' with it. The mistake was my dishonesty when she asked what happened because I was ashamed to admit the truth. All those mistakes added up to a bit of a friendship fallout."

Annie needed a regospeling reminder when that apron ripped. She needed to be reminded she was loved and cared for and that accidents don't make for defining moments. Peter and Paul needed that reminder too. And they weren't the only souls in the New Testament to ever need a bit of regospeling. Jesus took tons of time to remind people who he was and who they were.

It's not always easy being human, but it goes a lot better if we remember that we are humans who are loved, known, and forgiven.

WELCOME (5 MINUTES)

Welcome to Session 6 of *Believing Jesus: A Journey Through the Book of Acts*. To get things started, discuss the following question:

What's the worst part about a friendship ending?

VIDEO TEACHING (19 MINUTES)

Play the video teaching segment for Session 6. As you watch, use the following outline to record any thoughts or concepts that stand out to you.

Notes

To "regospel" someone means to remind that person of who he or she is and who Jesus is.

When we make a mistake, we can either back further away from intimacy with Jesus and try to clean ourselves up, or we can lean into him and let him clean us up.

Peter and Paul didn't just make mistakes *before* they knew Jesus but also while they were in relationship with Jesus.

For instance, almost immediately after Peter preached on the purity of the gospel in Acts 2—that it was faith in Jesus + nothing = salvation—Paul had to rebuke him for losing sight of the gospel (Galatians 2:11–21).

Then, right after Paul sets Peter straight for not living Christianly, he falls off the gospel wagon himself. In Acts 15, we see that Paul was a bit of a bullheaded leader when he got sideways with his best friend, Barnabas.

What is sad is that Paul's relationship with Barnabas is severed at this point, and we never again see Barnabas in all of Paul's amazing missionary journeys.

It was likely Paul's strong personality that caused the rift, because Scripture depicts Barnabas as a gentle man. Furthermore, if we look at all of Paul's life, we see a great man but certainly not a perfect one. He messes up and does not always walk in light of the grace of Jesus Christ.

We have to constantly preach the gospel to ourselves and to each other.

In fact, we need to get into the habit of regospeling ourselves, not to glorify our sins but to live out our salvation and remember that it is Jesus who does it for us.

SMALL GROUP DISCUSSION (30 MINUTES)

Take some time with your group members to discuss what you just watched and explore these concepts in Scripture.

1. What does it mean to "strip down" spiritually?

2. Why are we so often tempted to try to clean ourselves up instead of letting Jesus do it?

3. In Galatians 2:11–21, what was Paul's complaint against Peter? Why did he feel the need to set Peter straight?

4. Remember, this incident occurred shortly after Peter delivered his sermon in Acts 2 on the purity of the gospel. What had Peter lost sight of? What factors led him astray? What factors and situations likewise lead us away from the truth?

5. In Acts 9:26–27, we read that the disciples didn't trust Paul, but Barnabas did. What does that say about Barnabas' personality?

6. Knowing what you know about Paul and Barnabas and their personalities, how do you think their friendship lasted as long as it did?

7. What does it mean to be "regospeled"? How do we preach the gospel to ourselves?

8. What reminders of the gospel do you use or have in your life?

INDIVIDUAL ACTIVITY (5 MINUTES)

Spend the next couple of minutes thinking of your top four or five favorite Bible verses, the ones that remind you of who God is and who you are in Christ. When you get home, write each of them on a notecard. Pick one to memorize, and keep the card in your purse, your pocket, or in your car. Hang the other cards in the kitchen or bathroom so that you will be continually reminded of the truth.

CLOSING PRAYER

Thank You, God, for your Word. Help me to keep it close to my heart and always before my eyes. I want to live in a way that reminds me often to believe the gospel, believe that Jesus is who he says he is, and believe that I am who you say I am. Regospel me, Holy Spirit. Speak straight to my heart.

RECOMMENDED READING

Read chapter 8, "The Need to Be ReGospeled," in *Believing Jesus*. Use the space below to write down any notes or any questions you want to bring to the next meeting.

Between-Sessions Personal Study

Reflect on the content covered in the Session 6 group study by exploring the following material from the Bible and from *Believing Jesus*.

Day 1: Martha Was Human

The idea of being regospeled is that we are to constantly remind ourselves and each other — even in the midst of our mistakes and misunderstandings — that the gospel is true, that God is who he says he is, and that we are who God says we are. In these coming days of personal study, we will look at several stories from Scripture of people — real human beings with faults like us — who lost sight of this truth and had to be gently corrected. We will begin with two sisters, Mary and Martha of Bethany, both very different, both needing to be regospeled.

Read **Luke 10:38 – 42.** Why was Martha frustrated (verse 40)? What was her mistake?

Why was Jesus concerned about Martha? Why did he say Mary's choice was better?

What did Jesus do to regospel Martha? What truth did he remind her of?

Read **John 11:17–27.** This story takes place shortly after the death of Lazarus, the brother of Mary and Martha. Why do you think Martha went to meet Jesus while Mary stayed home?

How did Martha respond when Jesus said her brother would rise again? How did Jesus regospel her at this point?

Why do we often need to be regospeled during times of mourning?

In these two experiences, which of the following truths did Jesus remind Martha? Circle all that apply and cross out any that are absolutely not true.

The gospel is about rest.

The gospel is about freedom.

The gospel is about truth.

The gospel is about hard work.

The gospel is about compassion.

The gospel is about hospitality.

The gospel is about Jesus.

The gospel is about earning salvation.

The gospel is about resurrection.

The gospel is about new life.

Day 2: Mary Was Human

We're going to pick right up where we left off yesterday. Lazarus died and his sisters, Martha and Mary, waited four days before Jesus arrived. In fact, they had really hoped he would arrive in time to heal Lazarus.

Read **John 11:28–37**. What did Mary believe about Lazarus' death?

How did Mary's weeping affect Jesus?

In what ways did Jesus' actions regospel Mary more than his words? What does that mean to you personally?

Mary is the central character in another regospeling story, except this time she isn't the one being regospeled. Read **John 12:1–8**. What did Mary do to honor Jesus?

Why do you think Mary did that for Jesus?

How does this story show Mary's humanness?

How did Judas respond to Mary's act? What did Jesus say to Judas to regospel him?

Interestingly, a version of this story—a woman anointing Jesus—is found in each of the gospels. Scholars disagree on whether this is one story told four times or different events, but let's look at the details in each account. Read **Matthew 26:6–13, Mark 14:3–9,** and **Luke 7:37–39.** Checkmark in which gospel the details listed below are mentioned.

	Matthew	Mark	Luke	John
Jesus was in Bethany.				
Jesus was at Simon the leper's house.				
A sinful woman anointed Jesus.				
Mary anointed Jesus.				
A woman anointed Jesus.				
The woman brought an alabaster jar of oil.				
She poured the oil on his head.				
She wiped his feet with her hair.				
The oil was expensive.				
The disciples got mad at her for being wasteful.				
A Pharisee got mad at her for being wasteful.				
Judas Iscariot got mad at her for being wasteful.				
Jesus said she had done a beautiful thing.				
Jesus said this was preparing him for burial.				
Jesus regospeled all who were listening.				

Incredible, isn't it? The details shared at each event could point to it being either one singular event with four different perspectives, or multiple events. Most scholars lean toward Matthew, Mark, and John telling one story from three viewpoints and Dr. Luke telling a different one. Do you agree or disagree with that assessment? How many stories do you see told here?

One similarity in all the accounts is that Jesus reminded everyone listening of the beauty of sacrifice. What thoughts or questions do you have after reading all four accounts? How do you see Jesus using this opportunity speak truth to the people?

Day 3: John the Baptist Was Human

We meet John the Baptist early in the Gospels, practically before his father and mother do. As you might recall from the Session 1 personal study, John's birth was miraculous because his parents, Zechariah and Elizabeth, were "well along in years" (Luke 1:18). Regardless, the angel Gabriel told them that they would have a son, and he would "be filled with the Holy Spirit even before he is born" (verse 15).

Read **Luke 3:15 – 16**. John was now an adult preaching "a baptism of repentance for the forgiveness of sins" (verse 3). Who did people think John the Baptist was?

What did John say was the difference between himself and Jesus?

Read **Matthew 3:11–17**. What did John mean when he said the coming Messiah would "clear his threshing floor, gathering his wheat into the barn and burning up the chaff with unquenchable fire" (verse 12)?

Why didn't John want to baptize Jesus? Why did he finally relent?

Read **John 1:26–35**. What did John the Baptist shout when he laid eyes on Jesus? What did he testify in verse 34?

Read **Matthew 11:1–6**. Where was John the Baptist at this point? What two questions did John send his messengers to ask Jesus?

Jesus listed six things for the messengers to go back and report to John. Write them below.

1.

2.

3.

4.

5.

6.

Who was being regospeled in this story? Why did Jesus need to do this?

Take a minute to picture John the Baptist in your mind. At this point he is sitting in a dank jail cell, having given his entire life to prepare the way for Christ, and a few doubts have crept in. Has he sacrificed all this for the wrong man? Like us, he knows the truth (see John 1:34), but even when we know the truth, it is easy to listen to the whispers of doubt. How does this remind you that John the Baptist was human like us?

Read **Luke 7:24–33**. Even though Jesus had to regospel John the Baptist and remind him who he was, what did Jesus think about him?

What does this say about Jesus' heart for people who need a reminder of the truth?

Day 4: The Disciples Were Human

One gift of the four Gospels is that they each tell multiple stories of how human Jesus' best friends were. If we only had one gospel account, we might have a skewed view of some of Christ's followers, but having four gives us four different perspectives. Today's story, told in multiple gospels, reminds us of how Jesus had to regospel the disciples at times through his words and actions.

Read **Luke 9:1–2**. What did Jesus send the disciples out to do? What authority did he give them to accomplish this task?

Read **Luke 9:7–9**. This passage gives us, for just a second, a glimpse of the end of yesterday's story. Herod was confused about the identity of Christ, as some had told him Jesus was John the Baptist. In verse 9, what did Herod say in response to this claim?

That's right—Herod had John the Baptist beheaded (read the full story in Mark 6:17–29). John knew who Jesus was; he led the way and made straight the path (see Mark 1:1–3); and then he gave his life.

Read **Luke 9:10–17**. When the disciples returned, where did they all gather? Why did the people follow them there?

What was the disciples' concern when it grew late in the day? What was Jesus' solution?

Dr. Luke says "about five thousand men were there" (verse 14). How many people do you think could have been there in total, counting women and children? How much food did the disciples have to offer the crowd?

What did it look like for Jesus to regospel the disciples (verses 15–17)? How did this miracle remind them that Jesus was the Son of God?

Read **Matthew 14:13–21**. What differences do you see in Matthew's retelling of Jesus feeding the five thousand?

How many baskets of food were left over?

Jesus blessed the food, but the disciples were the ones who distributed the food to the people. What does this say to you about our role once we have been regospeled?

Read **Matthew 15:29–39.** How many people were following Jesus this time? For how many days had they been following him?

How much food did the disciples have to offer? What was their concern?

How much food was left over after everyone was fed?

Can you believe that just one chapter later, in a very similar situation (in fact, there were fewer people and more food this time), the disciples again needed to be reminded that Jesus was their miraculous provider? They needed to be RE-regospeled! When have you faced the same situation and needed to be reminded that Jesus is who he says he is and can do what he says he can do? Describe that time.

When we read about what the disciples did in the Bible and the works God performed through them, we can be tempted to think they were somehow superhuman. How do these stories remind us that the disciples were in fact very human, just like us?

Day 5: The Early Believers Were Human

Thus far, we have looked at individuals who knew Jesus and were *personally* regospeled by him. But Acts gives us glimpses into the lives of people who needed to be regospeled even though they did not personally know Jesus during his time on the earth.

In the Session 6 video, Lisa mentioned that right after the apostle Paul set Peter straight for not living in a Christian manner (see Galatians 2:11–21), he fell off the gospel wagon himself. Read **Acts 15:36–40**. What was the disagreement between Paul and Barnabas? What word is used in verse 39 to describe their disagreement?

In the original Greek, the word translated as "sharp disagreement" is *paroxusmos*, which means a provocation that literally cuts someone so they "must" respond. The word is used only one other time in the Bible. Read **Hebrews 10:24**. Which word or phrase do you think is the translation for *paroxusmas*?

In this verse, *paroxusmas* refers to spurring one another on. Crazy, huh? The same word that caused Paul and Barnabas to split ways—the same fierceness of disagreement—is the word for what the author of Hebrews encouraged us to do for fellow believers: Spur on. Push forward. Stir up. What are your thoughts when you see that parallel in Scripture?

Interestingly, this is the last mention of Barnabas in the book of Acts. He shows up in two of Paul's letters (1 Corinthians 9:6 and Galatians 2:13), but one has to wonder how much that friendship, and the severing of it, impacted Paul's life and writing. What a loss for Paul and the church because he didn't always walk in light of the grace of Jesus.

Read **2 Timothy 4:11**. What did Paul later say about John Mark? How does this show he was regospeled?

After Paul's split with Barnabas, he had the opportunity to regospel some of the new believers in Ephesus who had come to Christ. Read **Acts 19:1–7**. When Paul found these disciples, how had they been baptized?

As you'll recall from earlier in this personal study (and from Luke 3:16), with what two things does Jesus baptize a person?

How do you see Paul regospeling these disciples in light of this fact? What happened when they received that correction?

Read **Acts 19:8–12.** What do you think it looked like for Paul to regospel the followers of the Way when they were forced to move into the lecture hall of Tyrannus (verse 10)?

Read **Acts 19:22–41.** Where was Paul when this story was happening (verse 22)?

Why was there a riot in Ephesus? Who regospeled the crowd?

How was this conversation different than the others in this chapter?

Knowing that these are the people to whom Paul wrote the book of Ephesians, reading that letter as a tool of regospeling may change how you see it. Read **Ephesians 1:1–23**. How does verse 13 connect with Acts 19:1–7?

What are a few phrases Paul used in Ephesians 1 that sound like regospeling to you?

Which verse stands out to you? Why do you need to hear it in your life today?

Turning Your World Upside Down

(ACTS 5:17–42; 17:1–9)

INTRODUCTION

Do you know Jesus? Jesus, the divine hero who condescended to be clothed in flesh and born in a barn that very first Christmas? Jesus, who lived a perfect, sinless life so that his sacrificial death that very first Easter would have the power to reconcile mankind with our Creator? Jesus, the only One who's willing to lavish every single mistake-prone one of us with perfect, unconditional compassion that will never fade or fail? Do you know this Jesus?

FROM THE *BELIEVING JESUS* VIDEO

Annie writes:

"I don't know when you are reading this, but I am writing it during Holy Week—the week between Palm Sunday and Easter, the week where we see Jesus walk courageously to his death on our behalf. I have a lot of feelings during Holy Week. For some reason, more than usual, the story comes alive to me. I can follow his path for a week and see so many stops and connections and locations.

"Jesus stops being THAT Jesus from the pages, and he starts being THIS Jesus that changed everything for us. The book of Acts is about Jesus. To be fair, the entire Bible is about Jesus, but the book of Acts is about what happens when people believe that Jesus is who he says he is and can do what he says he can do. It's hard to turn a thin page in Acts and not spot the name of Jesus on it. This Jesus. King Jesus. The One to whom every other man and woman we meet in these chapters and verses gave their life. He gave their lives meaning and purpose and turned the world that he left upside down."

Holy Week reminds us of this Jesus, how it is all about him and how he is worth it all. This session will hopefully remind you of all that as well.

WELCOME (5 MINUTES)

Welcome to Session 7 of *Believing Jesus: A Journey Through the Book of Acts*. To get things started, just like in the video, take a minute to stand up and give quick shoulder massages to those on your right and on your left!

VIDEO TEACHING (20 MINUTES)

Play the video teaching segment for Session 7. As you watch, use the following outline to record any thoughts or concepts that stand out to you.

Notes

Song of Solomon 4:9 says that with one glance of our eyes, we captured God's heart. Our heavenly Groom is in love with us.

That same love that God lavishes on us must be what compels us to share about him with others.

If we view people as missionary projects, we are doing it wrong. We have to be compelled by compassion.

Peter, in his sermon in Acts 2, is the first to call Jesus "THIS Jesus" (verse 32). But Paul uses the phase in Acts 17:3 as well, when he teaches in Thessalonica about "this Jesus ... the Christ" (ESV). Paul is saying this guy, with the regular name, is the Messiah, the Anointed One.

A number of those in Thessalonica became believers as a result of Paul's preaching, and they were so passionate about the cause of Christ that they created a holy uproar. When the Jews dragged them before the city officials, they said, "These men ... have turned the world upside down" (Acts 17:6). These crazy Christians stepped on some toes.

The early believers were willing to suffer and be beaten with a cat-o'-nine-tails for the privilege to preach about Jesus. Right after receiving those thirty-nine lashes (the most Jewish law allowed), they said they were honored to be able to turn the world upside down.

In Philippians 2:10, Paul says that it is at the name of Jesus that every knee will bow. In John 14:6, Jesus says he is "the way, and the truth, and the life" (ESV). The early believers understood it is his name that carries so much power.

Dr. Howard Hendricks said, "Wherever Paul went, riots broke out. Wherever I go, people serve sweet tea." Can we identify with Dr. Hendricks? We need to be willing to get into a little trouble and turn the world upside down for the cause of Christ.

SMALL GROUP DISCUSSION (30 MINUTES)

Take some time with your group members to discuss what you just watched and explore these concepts in Scripture.

1. What is the significance of Paul saying in Acts 17:3, "This Jesus I am proclaiming to you is the Messiah"? What was he trying to get across to the Thessalonians?

2. What did it look like when Jason and the other new believers in Thessalonica were turning the world upside down for Christ? What did it look like when Peter, Paul, and the other early followers of the Way were turning the world upside down for Jesus?

3. In Acts 5:41, why were the apostles rejoicing after being beaten by the religious leaders? Why were they willing to suffer?

4. Why must we be driven by compassion instead of a sense of duty or obligation when it comes to sharing the truth about Christ?

5. How is grace and love for others different from mere tolerance?

6. What did Paul and the early Christians believe about the power of Jesus' name? How did that radically change the way they lived their lives?

7. How has the power of Jesus shaped and changed our lives? In what ways can we say we are willing to step on some toes, if necessary, to proclaim the message of Christ?

8. What would it look like for us to share about Christ wildly?

INDIVIDUAL ACTIVITY (5 MINUTES)

Think and pray about what it would look like for you to step on a few toes for the cause of Christ. Make a list of five ways you could step out in faith this week to boldly share the love of Christ with someone who needs to hear it and experience it.

1.
2.
3.
4.
5.

CLOSING PRAYER

Jesus, thank you for this story—for the whole book of Acts—that shows us what living the Christian life is about. We are grateful for your name, for the power we see it has in the lives of the apostles and early believers, and for the power we see it has now in our lives. Help us to be wildly brave for you and to turn our world upside down for your sake.

RECOMMENDED READING

Read chapter 7, "A Compassionate Compulsion," in *Believing Jesus*. Use the space below to write down any notes or any questions you want to bring to the next meeting.

Between-Sessions Personal Study

Reflect on the content covered in the Session 7 group study by exploring the following material from the Bible and from *Believing Jesus*.

Day 1: The Name of Jesus

As Lisa said in the Session 7 video, there is power in the name of Jesus. This is a power so great that it compelled the early believers—who were human just like us—to take risks, go to far-off places, brave punishment, and care for those in need. So during these days of personal study, let's take a look at this Jesus and see how his followers turned the world upside down.

Read **Matthew 1:18–25**. Notice that the angel of the Lord told Joseph exactly what to name the son who would be born to Mary. What is the significance of the name he would be given?

Jesus is the Greek form of Joshua or *Yeshua*, meaning "the Lord saves" or "Yahweh is salvation." Although that is Jesus' given name, the Bible gives him other names as well. Read Isaiah 9:6. What four other names is Jesus given?

1.

2.

3.

4.

Which of these names speaks to you right now? In what ways do you need Jesus' counsel? His might? His protection? His peace?

Take some time here to get a little artsy. Within the letters of Jesus' name below, doodle, draw, or write some other words that Jesus represents to you.

Read **Acts 3:6; 4:12; 8:12.** What do these three verses tell you about the name of Jesus?

Review **Acts 11:26.** The Greek word *Christos* is a translation of the Hebrew word *Mashach*, meaning "anointed." From this we get two titles for Jesus, God's anointed One: Christ and Messiah. How did this name give Jesus' followers their identity?

It's interesting to note Jesus' last name wasn't Christ, as we commonly refer to him today. In his own day, he would have been called *Yeshua Bar Yehosef* (Jesus, son of Joseph) or *Yeshua Nasraya* (Jesus of Nazareth). We see him referred to this way in John 6:42 ("Is this not Jesus, the son of Joseph") and John 18:4–5 ("'Who is it you want?' ... 'Jesus of Nazareth'"). As we will see during the Day 2 study, Jesus was a common name in Galilee at the time.

Day 2: THIS Jesus

It's funny to think that during New Testament times, Jesus was as common a name as John is today. It makes you wonder—did he have to be called Jesus C in school because Jesus Jacobson was in his class as well? In any event, with a name like Jesus, it makes sense there were times when he had to be identified in other ways besides just his first name. Yet he was also quite the standout, because he was not like any other Jesus. There is something powerful when we talk about THIS Jesus, as Peter conveyed in his first sermon.

Read **Acts 2:22.** How did Peter initially introduce Jesus? Why do you think he did this?

Read **Acts 2:32.** Why do you think Peter used the phrase "this Jesus"? Why did he need to separate our Jesus from any other Jesus?

This Jesus? He's not like any other Jesus. He's not like any other person who has ever walked this planet. Read **John 14:6**. How did Jesus label himself?

1.

2.

3.

What do each of those descriptions mean to you? Why does it matter that Jesus is the *way*? In your daily life, what does it mean that he is the *truth?* How does it impact you that he is the *life?*

Read **John 16:23–24**. What power did Jesus give his disciples to ask for things in prayer? What does it mean to come before God in the name of his Son, Jesus?

Read **Mark 16:17–18** and **John 14:12–13**. What power did Jesus give his disciples to do things in his name? How do the statements in these passages set "this Jesus" apart from anyone else?

Read **Acts 17:2–3**. Why did Paul use the phrase "this Jesus" here?

·Day 3: King Jesus

Of all the names that our Jesus—THIS Jesus—is given in Scripture, perhaps none is as important as his title of King. However, when the New Testament opens, we find that there is already a king on the throne of Israel: "After Jesus was born in Bethlehem in Judea, during the time of King Herod …" (Matthew 2:1). Herod was of Arab descent, but he had been raised as a Jew. He was a loyal supporter of the Roman government, which was in control of Palestine at the time, and because of these close ties he was able to get the Roman senate to declare him "King of the Jews." Like any power-hungry monarch of the time, it was a title he coveted, and he was none too willing to share that power or title with any other person.

Read **Matthew 2:1–12**. Who were the first people to call Jesus the king of the Jews? Why did that frighten King Herod?

What did Herod do to try to eliminate this threat? Why did his plan fail?

The words "kingdom of God" or "kingdom of heaven" are used more than 150 times in the New Testament. Often when Jesus taught, as in Matthew 13, he was teaching about how the kingdom of God runs and operates. Read **John 18:28–40**. What was Pilate's first question to Jesus? How did Jesus answer him in verses 36 and 38?

Jesus always knew who he was. He knew his name. He knew that when people referred to THIS Jesus, they meant him. He also knew that when he taught about the kingdom of God, it was the place where he reigned. Review Ephesians 1:18–22, which we explored in the Session 6 personal study. Why did Paul pray for the eyes of our hearts to be opened to Jesus' kingship?

What did Paul say about Jesus' kingship in comparison to any other ruler on earth?

Read **Philippians 2:9–11**. What authority did Paul say God gave to Jesus?

What will happen to the world at the sound of Jesus' name?

Read **Revelation 19:16**. When Jesus returns to earth, what name will be written on his thigh?

In **Daniel 2:37**, the prophet Daniel referred to King Nebuchadnezzar of Babylon as "the king of kings." What do you think this title meant? What does it mean when applied to Jesus?

The church in Acts clearly understood that Jesus was the King of an eternal kingdom, and it dramatically affected the way they acted and lived. As Lisa said in the video, there was something about this name—THIS King Jesus—that was worth turning things upside down for.

Day 4: Those Who Turned the World Upside Down

Paul was certainly one who turned the world upside down. Over and over again, he found himself in situations where speaking on behalf of the gospel caused a bit of an uproar. Let's look at some of these instances in today's Scripture.

Read **Acts 21:27–36** below. Circle every verb you see that relates to Paul's treatment.

> When the seven days were almost completed, the Jews from Asia, seeing [Paul] in the temple, stirred up the whole crowd and laid hands on him, crying out, "Men of Israel, help! This is the man who is teaching everyone everywhere against the people and the law and this place. Moreover, he even brought Greeks into the temple and has defiled this holy place." For they had previously seen Trophimus the Ephesian with him in the city, and they supposed that Paul had brought him into the temple. Then all the city was stirred up, and the people ran together. They seized Paul and dragged him out of the temple, and at once the gates were shut. And as they were seeking to kill him, word came to the tribune of the cohort that all Jerusalem was in confusion. He at once took soldiers and centurions and ran down to them. And when they saw the tribune and the soldiers, they stopped beating Paul. Then the tribune came up and arrested him and ordered him to be bound with two chains. He inquired who he was and what he had done. Some in the crowd were shouting one thing, some another. And as he could not learn the facts because of the uproar, he ordered him to be brought into the barracks. And when he came to the steps, he was actually carried by the soldiers because of the violence of the crowd, for the mob of the people followed, crying out, "Away with him!" (ESV)

The passage reads like a riot scene: the people of Jerusalem trying to kill Paul; the whole crowd stirred up against him and dragging him out of the temple; their shouting and uproar so great that he had to be carried to safety by the soldiers. Whoa.

Look again at verse 31: "As they were seeking to kill him, word came to the tribune of the cohort that all Jerusalem was in confusion" (ESV). Paul turned that city upside down for sure, and he hadn't even said anything yet! Just his presence caused chaos!

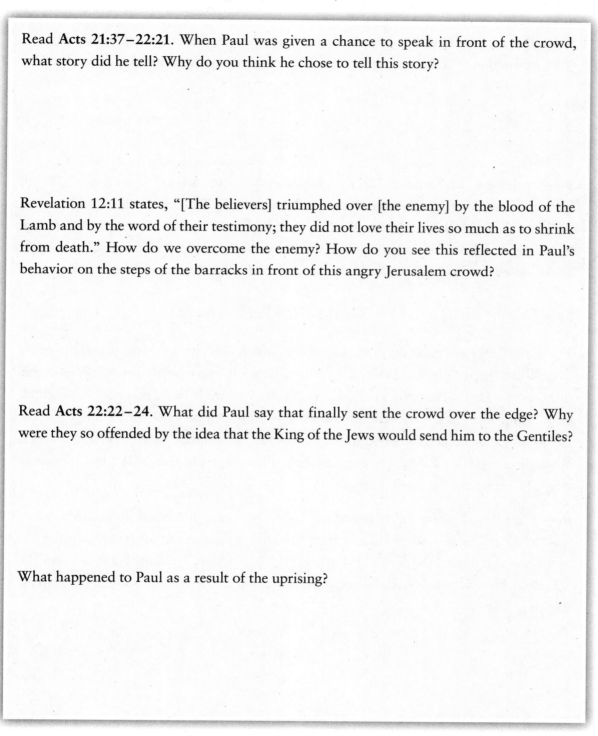

Read **Acts 21:37–22:21.** When Paul was given a chance to speak in front of the crowd, what story did he tell? Why do you think he chose to tell this story?

Revelation 12:11 states, "[The believers] triumphed over [the enemy] by the blood of the Lamb and by the word of their testimony; they did not love their lives so much as to shrink from death." How do we overcome the enemy? How do you see this reflected in Paul's behavior on the steps of the barracks in front of this angry Jerusalem crowd?

Read **Acts 22:22–24.** What did Paul say that finally sent the crowd over the edge? Why were they so offended by the idea that the King of the Jews would send him to the Gentiles?

What happened to Paul as a result of the uprising?

Read **Acts 23:11**. After all that mess—after everything had been turned upside down— what instructions did the Lord give Paul? Why do you think Jesus told Paul to be brave?

When you have some time today, read Hebrews 11. This chapter, known as the "Hall of Faith," describes a collection of people from the Old Testament whose faith turned their worlds upside down. Yet it's that first church of Acts—people like Paul, Peter, John, Dr. Luke, Barnabas, and our racial-reconciliation hero Philip—who turned the world upside down for the cause of Christ. What would it look like for us to be like them?

Day 5: We Can Turn Our World Upside Down

The New Testament believers caused a ruckus—with their stories, their plans, their very lives. What's incredible to consider is that the same Spirit who moved them and empowered them on that Day of Pentecost also lives in us. You've probably heard that before. But think on it again. The Holy Spirit who dwells within you remembers that first church in Acts. He was there on Pentecost. Stood by Stephen as he was stoned. Spoke to Peter in a dream about diversity. Gave Paul the strength to endure hardship. HE is in YOU, and because of this, YOU can turn your world upside down.

Remember from Session 1 that one of the last things Jesus instructed his followers to do was to "go and make disciples of all nations, baptizing them in the name of the Father and of the Son and of the Holy Spirit" (Matthew 28:19). We know from the book of Acts what this looked like for those early followers. What would it look like for you to go and make disciples?

What would it look like for you to turn your world upside down because of Christ? What are some things that would feel scary? Uncomfortable? Freeing? Joyful? Who would be involved? How would your life change?

As you read in Day 4, Paul was willing to turn his world upside down for Christ. Read **1 Corinthians 9:19–27**. What else was Paul willing to do to proclaim the message of Christ to the world?

What was Paul's motivation for doing this? What was his focus and goal?

It's the testimony of who Christ is in our lives and what he has done for us—THIS Jesus—that turns everything upside down. Through the power of the Holy Spirit, the lives of those around us can be changed by what Jesus has done in us. Look back at what we discussed about the work of the Holy Spirit in the Session 2 personal study. What does he do in our lives?

1.   The Holy Spirit _____.

2.   The Holy Spirit _____.

3.   The Holy Spirit _____.

4.   The Holy Spirit _____.

5.   The Holy Spirit _____.

When you think about everything the Holy Spirit does, how does it give you courage to share openly about who Christ is in your life?

Remember, it isn't just our words. Read **2 Corinthians 2:14–17**. What does Paul call all believers in this Scripture?

What does it mean to be the "pleasing aroma of Christ" (verse 15)? What does that indicate about your presence in a place?

Think about a candle burning in a room. If we like the smell, we are naturally drawn and attracted to it. In the same way, people are drawn to those who "smell" like Jesus. Do you know anyone like this in your life? Is there someone to whom you are drawn, and you know it is because of Jesus in them? Explain.

Write a prayer below, asking the Holy Spirit to move in you in such a way that it turns upside down the lives and hearts of the world around you.

Bearing the Chain Because

(Acts 28:16–31)

INTRODUCTION

The joy of watching other people's eyes widen and faces light up when they understood the gospel made all the unfair bumps and bruises Paul experienced along the way more than worth it. The difficult labor was worth the miraculous birth.

FROM *BELIEVING JESUS*

———

Annie tells this story:

"I went to a yard sale today with my best friend and her two kids. It was just a two-block walk, so she carried her ten-month-old while I held hands with her three-year-old. We shopped around for about half an hour and bought a plastic dump truck, a tiger costume, a set of five-pound weights, a set of three-pound weights, and a stuffed puppy.

"When it was time to head home, the three-year-old was in no mood for the trek. She didn't want to walk. She didn't want to *move*. My best friend had a ten-month-old in one arm, while in one arm I had sixteen pounds' worth of hand weights, toys, and clothes. Neither of us really had the ability to lift anything else.

"But my friend, though already weighed down, scooped up her daughter and carried her down the street. Though she struggled to walk, shifting the kids on her hips every thirty seconds, she was willing to bear the weight because of love.

"It's a simple example that reminds me of this last session. Sometimes love helps us bear things we normally wouldn't be willing to bear. That's what we have learned from these folks in Acts. From pain to shipwrecks to all manner of hard times, the members of the Way bore the chains because of their love for Christ."

So here we are at the end—one last week of study—watching as our Acts heroes suffer for the gospel and choose boldness in the face of fear or doubt or barriers. Let's end with that—the vision of those who bore the chains because of Christ.

WELCOME (5 MINUTES)

Welcome to Session 8 of *Believing Jesus: A Journey Through the Book of Acts.* To get things started, discuss the following question:

"It takes going to prison to set some people free." Do you think this statement is true? Why or why not?

VIDEO TEACHING (24 MINUTES)

Play the video teaching segment for Session 8. As you watch, use the following outline to record any thoughts or concepts that stand out to you.

Notes

It is incumbent on us as carriers of the gospel to be compassionate with those with whom we share it.

The gospel is true. Jesus died for us because he believed we were worth it. His resurrection power gives us power to boldly share the gospel and change lives.

In Acts 11:17, Peter explains the vision of the sheet descending from heaven and why he went into the house of Cornelius, a Gentile, and ate with him. He tells his critics, "If God gave them the same gift he gave us ... who was I to think that I could stand in God's way?"

In Acts 28:20, Paul, speaking from prison, says it was "because of the hope of Israel" (ESV) that he was in chains. To him, bearing the chain was no big deal, because the truth of Jesus' resurrection power—a power that brings life to that which is dead—was all worth it.

In Acts 28:30–31, we read that Paul lived in chains for two full years at his own expense. He preached the gospel boldly and without hindrance. He was willing to take any risk for the cause of Christ.

Do we believe God not only *can* do anything, but *will* do anything? This is the theme of the entire book of Acts—that our God chooses to work on our behalf. If we really believe this, we will take more risks for the sake of Christ.

If we recognize we have the power of the resurrection living inside us through the Holy Spirit, we will be compelled to reach our Judea and our Samaria with the love of Christ.

When we really get the love that the risen Christ has for us, it changes everything. We go from thinking we *can* see transformation in our world to thinking we *will* see it.

SMALL GROUP DISCUSSION (30 MINUTES)

Take some time with your group members to discuss what you just watched and explore these concepts in Scripture.

1. God has given us our personalities for a reason. How does that truth speak to our hearts?

2. How can we encourage each other in the unique ways God has made us? How can we encourage one another to operate in our giftings?

3. In the video, Lisa told the story of a young girl in Greece she calls "Priscilla," who had been rescued from human trafficking. How does Priscilla's story reveal the truth of the gospel and the power that Jesus brings to change lives?

4. How does Priscilla's story remind us that Jesus really is the King and that he not only *can* bring transformation to our world but also *will* bring it?

5. Think about Peter's statement in Acts 11:17: "Who was I to think that I could stand in God's way?" How have we been guilty of trying to stand in God's way when it comes to believing that he will bring change or do things for his kingdom in our world?

6. In what ways do we need God to change our thinking when it comes to sharing the love of Christ? How can we be more like the early Christians in Acts?

7. What does it means to be willing to "bear the chains" for Christ? How does Paul's story at the end of Acts help us to realize everything we endure for Jesus is worth it?

8. How has the love of Christ personally transformed us? In what ways are we not only believing Jesus but actually acting on those beliefs? How are we bringing God's kingdom into this world?

INDIVIDUAL ACTIVITY (5 MINUTES)

Do some brief brainstorming about how you (perhaps with a friend or other members of your study group) might demonstrate the love of Christ by "bearing the chains" for his sake. For instance, in light of Lisa's video story, you might check out organizations such as the A21 Campaign (http://www.a21.org/), research the work they are doing to set men and women free from slavery and trafficking, and then consider ways that you can act to help end the suffering of these victims. (For instance, you might consider becoming a member of A21's "A-Teams"—see the "Take Action" link on their site for more details.)

CLOSING PRAYER

Lord Jesus, open our eyes today to the truth of the gospel and its transforming power. Help us to believe, like the first Christians in Acts, that you not only CAN bring change but also WILL bring it. Let this truth impact our hearts and minds and affect every aspect of our beings. Help us to endure all things for your sake, take risks to advance your kingdom, and boldly turn our world upside down. May we never be the same because of what we have experienced in this study.

RECOMMENDED READING

Read chapter 9, "Bearing the Chain Because," and chapter 10, "Kicking Safe, Comfortable Christianity to the Curb," in *Believing Jesus*. Use the space below to write down any notes or questions from your reading, and take time this week to share these with a fellow group member. Reflect with that person on what you have learned from the early believers in the book of Acts and how your life has changed because of it.

Between-Sessions Personal Study

Reflect on the content covered in the Session 8 group study by exploring the following material from the Bible and from *Believing Jesus*.

Day 1: The Boldness of Priscilla

One of the stories Lisa told in the video was about a girl she named "Priscilla" who lives in a safe house in Greece. Lisa gave her this name because in the book of Acts, Priscilla was a gospel heroine who made many important contributions to early Christianity. She is a character well worth looking at if we want to see an example of boldness and the bearing of chains for the sake of Christ. So let's meet her today.

Read **Acts 18:1–4.** How did Dr. Luke identify Priscilla and her husband, Aquila? Why were they in Corinth?

The event to which Dr. Luke referred occurred in AD 49. When Christianity came to Rome, some of the Jewish synagogues there were open to the message of Jesus while others fought against it. The clash became so serious that the Roman emperor, Claudius, intervened and ordered the entire population of 40,000 to 50,000 Jews to leave the city. Priscilla and Aquila were among those forced to leave.

According to **Acts 18:3**, what did Priscilla and Aquila have in common with Paul? How do you think this affected their relationship?

How long did Paul stay in Corinth (verse 11)? If Paul chose to stay with Priscilla and her husband for that time, what does that tell you about their character and faith?

Read **Acts 18:18–19**. Why do you think Paul took Priscilla and Aquila along with him?

From what you know of Paul's time with them, why do you think he left them in Ephesus?

What have you learned, reading between the lines, about Aquila and Priscilla's ministry?

Read **Acts 18:24–26**. What kind of man was Apollos? For what did he need to be regospeled when it came to preaching about Jesus?

What was the difference between the baptism of John and the baptism of Jesus (see Acts 19:1–7)?

How was Priscilla a part of regospeling Apollos? What traits of boldness do you see in her character (especially given how women were treated in that culture)?

How sweet that Priscilla and Aquila together got the opportunity to regospel Apollos and encourage him. Their work would bear great fruit, for Apollos would eventually become an important leader in the church in Corinth (see 1 Corinthians 3:6).

Luke made no further mention of Priscilla and Aquila in Acts, but we do find references to them in Paul's letters. Read **1 Corinthians 16:19–24**. Why do you think the couple sent greetings to the Corinthians? What does that say about their relationship with that church?

Read **Romans 16:3–5**. What do you learn about Priscilla and Aquila in this letter from Paul to the church in Rome?

What do you think it looked like for Priscilla and Aquila to lead a church in their home (verse 5)?

Read **2 Timothy 4:9–22**. As we discussed in Session 3, Paul wrote this letter from prison. Based on these verses, what was Paul's mental state?

What is the significance of Paul's making sure to send a greeting to Priscilla and Aquila (verse 19)?

Why do you think Paul often wrote Priscilla's name first?

How would you describe Priscilla, based on these moments in Scripture?

Day 2: The Boldness of Peter

We have seen the power of Jesus' forgiveness in bringing out boldness in a person. As pointed out during the Session 2 personal study, Peter was certainly bold on the day of Pentecost when he gave a sermon in Jerusalem and three thousand people came to Christ, and his boldness continued to be displayed for much of the book of Acts. But today, let's look at the bold words he left behind for us.

Peter wrote two books that appear in New Testament. Scholars believe he wrote these letters to Christians living in the area of Turkey and Asia Minor who were being persecuted and suffering for their faith. Evidently, they were questioning whether God existed and whether he would protect them. The book of 1 Peter was written about four or so years before 2 Peter, so it's best to read them in order and see how Peter infused boldness into the believers.

If you have time, read both 1 Peter and 2 Peter—eight chapters total. As you do, you will see a caring and charismatic pastor encouraging his people to stay strong and never give up. In today's study, we will focus on just a few specific passages that highlight Peter's boldness.

Read **1 Peter 1:8–22** and recall what we have discussed during this study about Peter's past. To what degree do you think he could personally relate to the encouragement he was giving?

How did Peter know firsthand what it was like to endure trials?

How did the encouragement he gave strengthen his readers not to quit?

Reread verse 8. What do these words mean to you? How does Peter's boldness impact your life?

Read **1 Peter 2:9–10**. What did Peter mean when he stated, "Once you had not received mercy, but now you have received mercy"? How was this true in Peter's life?

Read **1 Peter 4:12–16**. Why did Peter say we should rejoice in our sufferings?

Why is it natural to question God when we are suffering?

Read **2 Peter 3:14–18.** Why was it important for Peter to boldly state the importance of Paul's letters to the people to whom he was writing?

Remember that Peter denied Christ three times with his words. How do you see the redemption he received in these letters? How does Peter's boldness to speak the truth of the gospel, even after he sinned, speak to you about your life?

Day 3: The Boldness of Paul

Much like our friend Peter, the apostle Paul underwent an incredible transformation in the book of Acts. Indeed, we have witnessed his power, boldness, and willingness to suffer for the gospel. He was so passionate about seeing Christ known around the world that he gave up everything. The thirteen letters he left behind served to shape not only the faith of the early believers but also the faith of all believers today.

What does the fact that Paul wrote these letters to help new believers (who were struggling with all kinds of issues) tell you about his boldness?

How would you describe Paul's global impact for the kingdom during the last two thousand years?

While Paul was under house arrest in Rome, he wrote a letter to a small church in Colossae. He had learned that false teachers were presenting philosophies to the believers that combined Christian, Jewish, and pagan beliefs but certainly wasn't the gospel. If you have time, read the entire letter to the Colossians (only four chapters). As we did in the Day 2 study, we will focus on just a few specific passages that highlight Paul's boldness.

Read **Colossians 2:1–5**. Why was Paul writing this letter? What did he hope to accomplish?

What "fine-sounding arguments" were influencing the Christians in Colossae? What are some "fine-sounding arguments" that have influenced the church today?

Read **Colossians 3:1–14.** How do you hear Paul's boldness in giving these instructions to the people of Colossae?

What does it mean to set your heart and mind on things above (verses 1–2)?

How do you clothe yourself with compassion, kindness, and humility (verse 12)?

How do you clothe yourself with gentleness? With patience?

Read **Colossians 4:2–6.** Why was Paul in chains? What did he ask the believers in Colossae to pray for?

Paul was willing to take risks to spread the message of Christ. Even though he was in prison, his one concern was that God would "open a door" so he could continue to preach the gospel! How can you, like Paul, boldly make the most of every opportunity to share Christ?

How can you be both bold and let your conversations be full of grace (verse 6)?

Day 4: The Boldness of Dr. Luke

During the course of this video study, you have likely gained a new love and appreciation for Dr. Luke. What a fantastic talent for research and writing, not to mention a real boldness to record these events for posterity (since he also lived through them!). Today's readings in the final two chapters of the book of Acts reveal some interesting things about the courage of Dr. Luke.

Read **Acts 27:1–12**. What does Luke's choice of pronouns (we, us, our) in this passage tell us about who was sailing for Italy?

Read **Acts 27:13–44.** The shipwreck we read about in this passage is often called "Paul's shipwreck," but according to that little word *we*, it was also Dr. Luke's shipwreck. It's amazing to read the story knowing that Paul and Dr. Luke were right there together for every scene in this dramatic account. What stands out to you about this shipwreck that Dr. Luke survived?

Why did Dr. Luke write down so many details?

Read **Acts 28:1–10.** What was Paul and Luke's experience on the island of Malta?

Read **Acts 28:11–31.** What does it say about Luke's boldness that he went with Paul all the way to Rome? Why do you think Luke braved all these trials and was willing to stay with Paul?

Read **Colossians 4:14.** We looked at this letter from Paul in Day 3's study, but what does he say about Luke in this verse? What does this tell you about the relationship between the two?

How did Luke describe Paul's preaching in Acts 28:31? How do you see Dr. Luke showing boldness even as he writes about Paul's boldness?

How has Dr. Luke's writing impacted your life? What questions would you ask him if you could?

Most scholars say that Dr. Luke never met Jesus in person. What do you think it was like for him to meet Jesus in heaven?

Day 5: The Boldness of Jesus

There is no better place to end this study than on focusing on the One whom this book is about—THIS Jesus. King Jesus. Our Jesus.

In the space below, write 10 words or phrases you would use to describe Jesus based on what you have learned.

1.

2.

3.

4.

5.

6.

7.

8.

9.

10.

Read **Philippians 2:5–8**. How did Paul describe what Jesus did for us in this passage? How does that illustrate his boldness in coming to this world?

Read **Philippians 2:12–18.** How does Paul encourage us to be like Jesus?

What does it mean to "work out your salvation with fear and trembling" (verse 12)?

Going forward from this study, what would it look like to continue to regospel yourself and continue to work out your salvation?

What was your biggest revelation during this study about the character of Christ, his boldness, and the effect he had on the followers of the Way?

How have you seen Christ change Peter's life and give him boldness?

How have you seen Christ change Paul's life and give him boldness?

How have you seen Christ change Dr. Luke's life and give him boldness?

How have you seen Christ change the lives of other early believers—Philip, Stephen, and Priscilla—and give them boldness?

How has your view of the Holy Spirit changed during this study?

Copy Philippians 2:12–13 below, and read the words as if Paul were writing them straight to you. Then write a prayer, sealing the work the Holy Spirit did in your life through this study.